How to Start a Successful Business

Professor Russell Smith
Business Boffins
Oxford UK

www.businessboffins.com

First published 2007 by Boffins House Publishing, part of Business Boffins Ltd
Business Boffins Ltd
Dairy Barn, Belcher's Farm, High Street Little Milton, Oxfordshire, OX44 7PU
www.businessboffins.com
email fiona@businessboffins.com

British Library Cataloguing in Publication Data
A catalogue record for this book is available from the British Library

ISBN- 978-0-9555501-1-9

Produced by Boffins House Publishing
Book design and layout by Nine Creative Ltd, Milton Keynes
Printed and bound in Great Britain by Ashford Colour Press, Portsmouth

Let's be honest: there's an astonishing amount of business information currently available. But despite that, business success in the UK isn't as good as it should be. In fact, more than half of all businesses fail in their first three years. We can, and must, do better. The problem for anyone new to business is how to identify the *wisdom* hidden amongst all of the *information* that's available.

Wouldn't it be really useful if someone could come up with a common sense approach that set out all of the essential stuff that you need to know, presented in a logical sequence? Perhaps by bringing together a team of experts? Maybe professional advisers (accountants and lawyers *etc*), bank managers and experienced business owners? And then, just to be extra safe, wouldn't it be great if all of that material was checked and accredited by a University Business School? Better still, how about testing that material with around 150 businesses over their first year of trading? The Business Boffins team thought that would be a good idea. So we did it.

We did a lot more besides: intensive research about the needs of business owners in the planning stage, at the business launch, as they got to grips with running their business and then as they planned for growth. And, from nearly 2,500 conversations, we found them the answers to all of their questions as they arose. All of which really made a difference. We know because they told us: in an anonymous poll our programme received a 95% approval rating. And our approach radically improved business survival.

That was back in 2003. Now we've taken all of the important stuff that made a difference, combined it with the answers to questions that business owners asked, and distilled it into three books that explain how to start, run and grow a successful business. It's all taken a lot of work — which probably explains why we can't find anyone else who has done this. But it does mean that we can say, with great confidence, that if you want to start a successful business then we can really help.

Professor Russell Smith
Oxford, April 2007

Contents

If you want to start a successful business, then this is the stuff that you need to know. If you are new to business do look out for business terms that are unfamiliar — these are explained in a straightforward way in the Glossary. Many of the chapters include case studies and business profiles of which some are drawn from businesses featured in "The Independent" or "The Independent on Sunday".

Chapter		Page
1	Introduction	9
2	What are you going to sell?	23
3	Do you have a market?	35
4	Your business structure	49
5	Protecting your ideas	61
6	Professional advisers	73
7	Tax, National Insurance and VAT	83
8	Basic accounting	93
9	Premises and equipment	107
10	Risk and insurance	119
11	How to budget	131
12	Writing your business plan	145
13	Sources of finance	167
14	Raising finance	177
15	Finding and employing people	189
16	Launching your business	201

Appendices

	Page
Glossary of business terms and acronyms	211
Index	216
Sponsor details	222
About the author	226

Enterprise, the process of running a business, is exactly that: a process. And since any process can be broken down into a series of tasks, it can be learnt. What this book cannot teach are the skills needed to make a product or deliver a service — those things that you want to sell. That's your bit; whether you are a plumber, a florist, a wedding planner, a web designer, a painter and decorator or even an inventor. And so we have to assume that you have those 'technical skills' already. What this book *will* teach you about are the 'enterprise skills' needed to plan and start your business.

> Every business must sell something (either a product or a service) and every business must make a profit

Lesson number one, is that you should stop thinking of yourself in terms of your technical skills. You may, for example, be a qualified plumber but from now on we want you to start thinking like a business person. That doesn't mean trying to behave like Sir Richard Branson! In any case, that stuff comes later in Book 3: "Growing a successful business". What we mean is having business principles at the front of your mind all of the time. Above all, we want you to make a profit. And not, of course, by ripping off customers or forgetting to pay your tax bills. That's cheating (a bad thing). And no fun (a very bad thing).

Now every business must sell something. But if its costs are greater than its sales income then the business will get into trouble. And so your business must be able to pay all of its bills, including the wages bill, and still make a profit. So don't 'fake' a profit by taking lower wages than you actually need. You'll only be fooling yourself. And don't get hung up about the 'P' word: profit. Making a profit is essential for business survival. What you spend that profit on is up to you. We don't care if you give the profit to charity or spend it on cocktails in The Bahamas. That's entirely up to you. By the way, if you choose the latter option then Johnny Canoe's restaurant in Nassau is worth a visit. Sorry, digressing a bit.

Anyway, the secret of increasing your chance of business success is simple: get the plan right to start with. If the plan doesn't work, enterprising people (like you) make a new plan. People that can't do that are called 'employees'…

So you want to start a business? Well, it seems only fair that we tell you straight away that it isn't easy: more than half of all businesses cease trading in the first three years. But the really sad fact is that most fail due to avoidable reasons. This book, aimed at getting you off on the right track, will help you *avoid the avoidable*.

There are many reasons why people start their own business. Some people take the plunge after dreaming about it for years. Others grab an opportunity that comes along unexpectedly such as redundancy. Perhaps one of the most common reasons is quite simply the idea of *freedom*.

- **Freedom to be your own boss**
- **Freedom to do what you love doing**
- **Freedom to work with people you like**
- **Freedom to work when you want to work**
- **Freedom to be happy**

Well... dream on. Here's what to expect:

- **Freedom to work very long hours**
- **Freedom to be unpopular with your partner**
- **Freedom to be chasing people who don't pay**
- **Freedom to spend hours doing paperwork**
- **Freedom to deal with clients on Sundays**

So why on earth do it? Simple: because it is absolutely, mind-bogglingly brilliant when you make it work. A sense of satisfaction you've not felt since you ate all the chocolate in your Christmas stocking (before breakfast) without being sick. And that wonderful feeling, that there's no really good word for, when you run into your old school teacher who said you'd never make anything of yourself...

Remember me, Mrs Woods?

In 2007 it was estimated that the UK had almost four million active businesses in total. The government splits up these businesses according to size:

Government Category	Number of people
Small	less than 50
Medium	50–249
Large	250 and above

An important sub-division is the so-called "micro business" that has less than 10 employees since this is where a lot of growth has been seen in recent years. However, large companies account for almost half of the turnover (sales income, not profit) in the UK. And so there must be loads of big businesses, right? Wrong: there are less than 7,000 in the UK and small businesses account for 99% of the total. However, research does show that employing people improves the chance of business success - it probably makes a business more efficient since the paperwork needed for a one-person business isn't nine times less than that for a business with nine people! In fact, a recent survey of small business owners showed that they worked an average of 63 hours per week, with 16 hours spent on administration. You don't need to be a genius to work out that help with administration could be of real value, therefore, to lots of businesses. And an experienced book-keeper can probably do in eight hours what it might take the rest of us 16 hours to do.

We think that the first question to ask is 'what exactly do you want to achieve?' Are you looking to build a business that will fund all of your family expenses? Do you have a hobby that you'd like to turn into a part-time business? Do you want a business that will grow and be something that you can pass on to your children? Or do you want to sell the business, after you've built it up, and use the money to retire on? **Don't be afraid to be selfish here — it's your business, what do you want to achieve?** Let's take a look at a couple of case studies to illustrate how to define the key aspects of your own business idea.

Edward Johnson was an accountant with a London-based company. His daily commute took two hours each way and he was missing his family growing up. Eddie had the chance of redundancy and he planned to set up a small practice and attract private clients. He felt confident since he already helped friends with their tax returns. He had a skill that was marketable, could work from home and had a number of potential customers. Eddie spent the evenings over the next three months planning out what he would do to launch his business. Cash would be tight at first but he received a reasonable redundancy settlement to carry him through. We can summarise this case study, very simply, as follows:

Driving reason:	**Lifestyle change**
Product/service:	**Accounting services**
Start-up cash:	**Minimal requirement**
Sales/Income:	**Acceptable**
Work/life balance:	**Favourable**

CASE STUDY: STEVE MELLOWS, THE CAR MECHANIC

Steve Mellows worked for a garage and Jan Mellows managed a high-street store. With three young sons, Mr and Mrs Mellows wanted to earn more in order to buy a larger home. They decided that Steve should set up a mobile car repair business in order to achieve a bigger income. Steve handed in his notice and bought a van and some essential tools with the savings that they had in the bank. It was a struggle right from the start. They had no spare cash to spend on advertising which meant that work was slow for the first three months. Steve found himself working evenings and weekends. After six months the Mellows family found themselves in debt. Steve returned to full-time employment in order to get a loan to pay off their debts. Once again, we can summarise this case study using the same five categories that we used in the previous example:

Driving reason:	**Financial**
Product/service:	**Car repair services**
Start-up cash:	**Used all bank savings**
Sales/income:	**Unacceptable**
Work/life balance:	**Unfavourable**

WHAT CAN WE LEARN?

Edward the accountant behaved in an enterprising manner whilst Steve the mechanic did not. For example, Edward took a close look at what his financial requirements were, researched whether there was a market for his services and spent three months planning out how he would launch his business. As a result of that careful planning he was able to create a business that would generate the required income and also gave a favourable work/life balance. By contrast, Steve had a good business idea but made the classic mistake of launching with inadequate cash reserves. Too little planning and a lack of market research were also major faults. He could, for example, have remained in full-time employment whilst he did his market research. To do that, he could have hired a van, just on Saturdays, and offered a mobile car repair service such that people got their cars repaired on a day that they didn't need their car for work. After, say, three months of that experience Steve would have been in a much better position to judge whether to go it alone on a full-time basis. And, when he did go ahead, it may have been better to lease a van rather than blow his cash on buying one — cash that could have been used for advertising needed to launch and grow his business.

PLANNING YOUR BUSINESS

Whilst these examples may seem rather obvious, you would be amazed at how frequently new businesses make the same classic mistakes again and again. It's therefore, in our view, impossible to overstress the need for careful planning before you start your business. Many start-up advisers will ask you to complete long questionnaires in order to help assess whether you have what it takes to turn your idea into a viable business. That can be very helpful. But we ask that you consider just the five questions that we used to summarise the previous case studies.

1 *Driving reason:*	**Why are you doing this?**
2 *Product/service:*	**What will you sell?**
3 *Start-up cash:*	**How much will you need?**
4 *Sales/income:*	**What income do you need?**
5 *Work/life balance:*	**Will this be acceptable?**

So questions 1 and 5 are *personal* ones, questions 2 to 4 in the middle are *business* related; this is our **"Start-up Sandwich"**. If taking a bite at this doesn't taste right then you should probably stop now. Let's look at this in a little more detail.

1 Driving reason: What is your main reason for starting a business? Be honest - this is your life! Do you simply want a business that will 'provide a living' or do you want to develop a business that you will later sell and make a 'capital gain'?

2 Product/service: Business is very simple - people buy things from you whether that is something that you make or a service that you offer. What is your product or service? How will you make it or provide it? What premises will you need? Will you need to employ other staff? Can you develop a range of products or services?

3 Start-up cash: How much money will you need just to start? Will you need to invest in expensive equipment? What budget will you need for advertising? How much money will you need to cover the early period before you are selling your product? These are just some of the questions to consider as you start planning.

4 Sales/income: Is there a market for your product? Will anyone want to buy it? Can you sell as much as you need in order to provide the income that you require?

5 Work/life balance: Will running your own business offer a reasonable balance between work and the rest of your life? Do you have the support of your family and your friends? Ultimately, will you be happier if you run your own business?

Addressing these five simple areas isn't as easy as you might think. There are lots of hidden issues to consider and there is no real alternative to undertaking a proper planning exercise. On the face of it, that appears quite complicated. But breaking it down into chunks makes it much easier. *And that is exactly what we do with the chapters that follow.*

Whatever your reasons for starting a business they are probably not as dramatic as those cited by John Jones, the founder of **Protek-Dor Ltd,** a lorry driver who was the victim of two gas attacks. John invented devices that make lorry cabs safer for drivers. However, John and Debbie Jones faced a number of issues as they developed their business of which the key one was finance. Luckily, they were able to use the format for the business documents that you'll read about later. They had a good product and raised the finance needed from investors. Take a look at their story in the Business Profile.

John Jones is a former truck driver based in Banbury, Oxfordshire. Together with Debbie Jones he started **Protek-Dor Ltd** *in 2001.*

People offer many reasons for starting a business. But being gassed? That's a new one. Yet that was exactly what prompted John and Debbie Jones to start their own company, Protek dor Ltd. "Attackers used tubing to feed a toxic gas into my cab whilst I slept", explained John. "Being gassed once was bad enough but being gassed a second time, some months later, made me think seriously about what could be done to protect drivers."

And so trucker turned inventor John came up with two devices: 'Kab-gard', that protects the cab door window, and 'Lok-gard' that secures the door handle and lock against attack. Truckers loved the products. Ian Swanwick of John Blackstock Transport said, "I stopped for a coffee before crossing the border out of Spain and when I returned to my truck I caught three men trying to break the locks. There is no doubt that if the Lok-gards had not been in place I would have been returning to either an empty vehicle or no vehicle at all."

Initial funding for the venture came from around £30,000 of John and Debbie's savings together with a business loan for another £30,000 using the family home as security. The problem for the business was that generating income was difficult without first having the cash to order large production runs of product and to fund a sales campaign. The business had reached a critical point in its development — *it needed to raise finance to fund growth.*

Since the company had real growth potential, the solution was to raise equity finance through the sale of shares (or equity) to investors. In order to do that the company needed 'investor ready' business documents. These documents, the 'holy trinity' of all equity financings, are: a business plan, a cash flow forecast and a funding presentation.

Debbie Jones got professional help with these key documents and then approached potential investors. Ted Mott, founder of Oxford Capital Partners, liked what he saw and set about helping the business secure long term development funding.

A substantial injection of cash, from equity finance, will help the business to reach its full potential. But that comes at a price. By selling shares in their business, Debbie and John Jones will have to make room for other people in the decision-making process. However, the best 'Business Angel' investors usually have vital business experience to offer and will lend credibility to your business.

This case study first appeared in "The Independent on Sunday"

With so much to think about, you'd be forgiven for thinking that it must have been really difficult for John and Debbie Jones to know where to start with their business. For example, they needed to protect the invention with a patent. And then find someone capable of manufacturing the products. Plus there was the big issue of financing the business. And, of course, they needed to market the products effectively. So their business plan must have been hugely complicated? Well, there was a lot to think about and to include in the business plan. But by breaking down everything into sensible chunks it made writing the plan much easier, as explained below.

DEVELOPING YOUR OWN BUSINESS PLAN

Many people find the task of writing a business plan, and the associated cash flow forecast (*your business budget*), quite daunting. The chapters of this book have therefore been arranged in a logical sequence so that you'll be able to plan your business effectively. And, we hope, develop the components for your written business plan as you go along. The next figure illustrates the approach that we take. It is based on a logical sequence that starts by defining what you are going to sell (your product or service), whether you have a market and what would be the appropriate business structure for you.

Next, we look at whether you need to protect your ideas (perhaps with a patent) and what professional advisers (patent attorneys, accountants, solicitors *etc*) you will need. After that, the chapters cover the basics of business accounting including sections on tax, national insurance, VAT and

formal accounting. This last bit isn't as bad as it sounds! After that, we really start to get to grips with your business idea by looking at premises and equipment as well as risk and insurance. Once we've assembled most of the components of your business plan, the next chapter brings it all into context by explaining how to set about drafting your own document. And the business plan shouldn't be more than 30 pages long. We are not looking for something the size of a telephone directory, just a common-sense summary of what your business is all about.

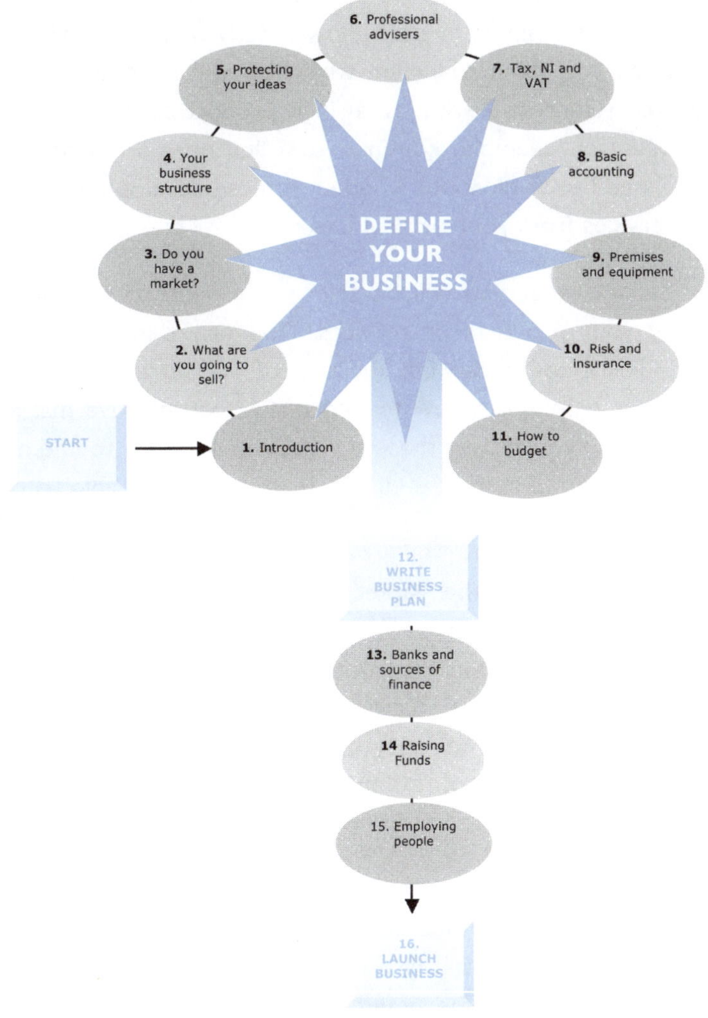

A key part of the plan is the business budget (cash flow forecast); a financial tool that looks at money coming in and out of your business on a monthly basis. You need access to the EXCEL spreadsheet package from Microsoft to help with this. This forecast is a vital part of the planning process since it will enable you to determine whether your business idea is viable. After that, it's on to writing the business plan itself. With those documents completed, the final chapters look at banks and sources of finance, employing people and launching your business which is what this is all about. Well that's the end of this introduction. Let's now take a look at the building blocks shown above, and covered in the following chapters, in more detail.

Chapter Two focuses on what you are going to sell. All businesses must sell something, be it a product, a service or a combination of the two. And really smart business owners know exactly what they sell. But it's not as easy as you think to define what you will be selling. Few businesses are really successful with just a single product or service (even eBay and Google, for example, continue to offer new products and services). You'll need to think about whether you can develop a range of products and services from your original idea.

Once you've defined what you will be selling, you need to find out if anyone will buy your products or services. You may think that your product is wonderful, and cheap, but the rest of the world might not! Chapter Three will explain how to undertake cost-effective market research that will help you answer these key questions. Better to find out early on if there is a good market — if not, then you will be able to re-think your products and services before launching your business.

Once you feel confident about the market opportunity then the next step is to decide on what kind of business structure is appropriate for you. It may be that you prefer to work on your own or with others in a partnership. Both structures carry liability issues. Some liabilities can be avoided by setting up a limited company or a limited liability partnership. There are pros and cons to all of the options and Chapter Four will help you to decide the best type of business structure for you.

Once you've decided what you want to sell, to whom and under what business structure it's worth considering if you need to protect your ideas before you go any further. If you have an invention then maybe you need a patent? Perhaps you have some 'brand' names that you wish to trade mark? The outward appearance of your product may be important and you may need to register a 'design right'. Or it might just be a matter of keeping things secret — Chapter Five will help you to decide.

If you need to protect any of your ideas then, in addition to a solicitor, you may also need a patent attorney. Of all professional advisers, we think that an accountant is the most important one. Accountants can help you plan your business. They can help you manage your business as well. And they can be invaluable if you need to raise finance from the bank. But there are lots of other advisers that you might need. Chapter Six looks at the key advisers used by all forms of business.

Tax, national insurance and VAT aren't the most interesting topics perhaps. But you'll need to understand how these things work if you want to start your own business. The good news is that there's lots of information available from government agencies. And your accountant can do much of the work for you — but at a price. **Chapter Seven** explains what is involved, what you should be doing yourself and what your accountant could do that would be cost-effective for you.

You'll need to deal with many people in business who speak a foreign language: finance. Getting to grips with finance and accounting will not only allow you to speak their language but also make it easier for you to run your business. You'll be able to have more effective meetings with your accountant. And that will save you time and money. And you'll be more likely to get a bank loan should you need one. So don't 'speed-read' **Chapter Eight** as you really need to know this stuff.

All businesses need to think about premises and equipment, even if you work from home. The costs associated with premises and equipment can be very high and may form a substantial component of your 'start-up' costs. Understanding what your options are, what the practical requirements are and what your legal responsibilities will be are all vital components of putting together a good plan for your business. **Chapter Nine** covers all of these issues and will help get you on the right track.

Just like road tax for a car, businesses have to take out certain forms of insurance by law. Understanding the risk in your business is the first step towards looking at how you may wish to insure against that risk. In particular, you are the most important asset in your business — what would happen if you fell ill for a long period of time or had an accident. **Chapter Ten** looks at the common forms of protection and will help you to decide what is needed (not just 'nice to have') for you and your business.

Chapter Eleven shows you how to develop and create a cash flow forecast. This simple spreadsheet — best done with a package such as Microsoft's EXCEL — allows you to forecast what money will comes in and out of your business. Quite simply, this is the cash flow through your business. It allows you to see what your start-up costs will be and if you need start-up funds via a bank loan. It also allows you to check, month-by-month, whether your business is performing once launched.

Chapter Twelve is really at the heart of this book. Understanding the process of planning a business is really important if you want to create a sound business plan. It's no use just copying things from a high street bank booklet – you really need to understand the philosophy of business planning and how business plans can evolve with time. And you need to know how to ensure that everything ties in with the cash flow forecast — the budget associated with your business plan.

Most businesses will need some cash to get going. Perhaps to fund the purchase of a computer and office equipment. Or to fund the purchase of raw materials. Or even to fund the costs of a patent. Whatever your business idea, it is unlikely that you'll have no requirement for start-up funding. Chapter Thirteen looks at sources of finance and explains how to secure the funds that you need whether that is via equity finance (selling shares to investors) or debt finance (loans from banks).

The process of raising finance is covered in Chapter Fourteen. This chapter looks at what bankers will want to know when assessing a loan application. It also covers the investment process all the way through from private "business angel" investors through to the professional Venture Capital companies. Useful for those new to business will be the section that explains how to prepare a funding presentation for bankers and investors. This format has proved successful in helping lots of business owners to raise many millions of pounds of finance in real life.

Many businesses start with just the founder but quickly recognise that employing other people — even on a part-time basis — can be hugely beneficial. For that reason, you need to know how to define the kind of person that you need — a job description — and how to interview people against that specification. And you also need to know some of the basics about employment law. Chapter Fifteen will guide you through the employment issues that all business owners must understand.

This is the time to pop the champagne cork — the launch of your own business. Getting the launch right is a vitally important component of starting a successful business. Anyone can spend thousands on advertising — the trick is to ensure that your marketing works! Chapter Sixteen explains what to do in order to ensure an effective launch for your new business. Of course, the next step is to manage and grow your business, topics covered in the next two books in this series.

Anyway, that's what to expect as you read further. But, in the meantime, here are ten useful things for you to be getting on with <u>now</u> as you read through this book:

1 **GET FREE HELP:** Attend one of the free Business Link start-up courses or seminars local to you (www.businesslink.gov.uk) both for information and to learn from other new business owners. If you need premises for your new business then speak with a Business Link Adviser about local options.

2 **DEFINE WHAT YOU WILL SELL:** All businesses must sell a product, a service or a combination of the two. Look to see if you can sell variants of your original idea in order to create a range of products or services.

3 **DO YOUR MARKET RESEARCH:** And don't be afraid of competition, it shows that there is demand. Be objective — don't just talk with friends.

4 **TEST YOUR BUSINESS IDEA:** Can you test your idea by working evenings or weekends before leaving employment and committing to it full-time?

5 **TALK TO SUPPLIERS:** If your business will need to buy from suppliers, start talking to a range of them now. Identify two suppliers for everything you will need. Get their price lists — these are helpful for your cash flow forecast.

6 **INTERVIEW ADVISERS:** Visit three accountants that specialise in small business services and select one. Ask your accountant about help with (i) registrations for tax and national insurance, (ii) calculating monthly payroll and, (iii) VAT returns (if appropriate). Get their advice on how to do book-keeping in a way that will be helpful to them when they do your tax returns.

7 **FIND AN INDEPENDENT FINANCIAL ADVISER:** Have an initial meeting with an Independent Financial Adviser to find out options for, and costs of, pension schemes and any likely insurance needs.

8 **BUILD A RELATIONSHIP WITH THE BANK:** If you need start-up finance (a loan or an overdraft) then ask your accountant (see 7) to recommend a good bank manager. Most banks offer similar services and so the personal relationship often becomes the key factor in choosing a bank but still…

9 **VISIT FIVE HIGH STREET BANKS:** Grab their 'start-up' guides and compare the services that banks offer. Try and speak with a bank adviser.

10 **TRY TO SET SOME CASH ASIDE:** Although very difficult for most people, do consider setting aside some cash to at least cover mortgage payments for three months. Don't lose your home.

These early chapters all lead to the preparation of a business plan. But there will be no business plan, and certainly no business, unless you have something to sell. All businesses must sell products or services in some shape or form. So, quite deliberately, we want you to think about your product(s) and/or service(s) first. To make life simple though, let's just call it a "product" whatever you intend to sell. And just so you are clear about how important your product is, remember that businesses often fail for one of two common reasons:

- **the business sold less products than it needed to do in order to make a profit**

- **customers didn't pay for the products that they had bought from the business**

> **Businesses usually fail because they sell too little or because they don't get paid on time**

Really good businesses often combine sales of a product with additional services. Such additional services might relate to:

- the **point of sale** — perhaps an excellent delivery service

- **after-sales services** — perhaps an information hotline that you can telephone for any help that you need

We took a look in a dictionary of business terms (we won't 'name and shame') to find a definition of the word 'product' in the *business* sense. To our astonishment this Business Dictionary, first published in 1970 and reprinted loads of times since, didn't include that word. To our way of thinking, that is a fundamental omission but perhaps explains why so many businesses fail in the UK.

People simply forget that a business is all about selling a product. Without selling a product your business will fail. Now this may all sound a little repetitious. Good. We want this message to go home loud and clear:

To be successful in business, indeed simply to survive in business, you must sell a product and you must make a profit (ie more cash must come into the business than goes out of the business over a period).

There are many ways in which people label what they do or what their business does. For example, James Dyson says that he makes vacuum cleaners. So it's obvious that he knows what his product is. And it's also obvious that his business is successful. So James Dyson (or rather, his business) makes a product, in his case a vacuum cleaner. But some other people in business don't make their products at all; their product is what they do for other people. Some kind of 'service product'. By the way, that same dictionary of business terms didn't have a definition of the word 'service' either. We wish we could tell you that we were making this up. But we aren't. It does contain a definition of, 'Inland Waterways Amenity Advisory Council' though. So that's good.

CASE STUDY: SERVICE PRODUCTS

Anyway, what is a service product? Well, you could say that a plumber offers a service. That service might be to fix a leaking radiator valve. Well, that's what we thought anyway. We had a leaking valve in the office and called a plumbing firm (Company A). They told us that they don't do leaking valves. "You need a domestic plumber mate", came the rather curt response. So we found one (Company B) and called them up. "It's a £75

minimum call-out fee plus parts" was the reply. We thought we'd buy a valve and fit it ourselves. Which we did. It cost £6.75. And then £263 (plus VAT) to replace the carpet that got ruined by the rusty water that gushed all over the office floor. So actually company 'B' aren't only plumbers — *they sell a carpet protection service*. Well, this may sound like a joke but it does have a serious message which is that it's very important to know what you are selling. And to know what you are selling *from the customer's point of view*. For plumbing company 'B', when we looked closely at their advert it included the phrase, "Fully Insured". An important point. It meant that had the carpet been ruined by them then it wouldn't have cost us anything to replace it.

Oh well. We learnt our lesson.

Another example comes from a business called 'ABC Tree Surgeons' (*we changed the name before you reach for the phone book*). There was a big old ash tree in my garden that needed to be felled in order to make way for a new building extension. Turning to "Yellow Pages", I found the business and was attracted to the fact that their advert proclaimed, rather proudly, "Insurance cover to £5 million". "Must be a professional outfit", I thought and called them straight away. The tree was felled the following week. Reflecting afterwards, I realised that the service I had bought wasn't simply cutting down the tree; it was cutting it down professionally and safely and in a way that wouldn't cause a rift with my neighbour if an accident had happened. And even if an accident had happened, there was ample insurance cover to sort out any damages to my property or to that of my neighbour.

Incidentally, being a wood-worker in my spare time, I had the same company convert the logs into planks that I now have drying ready to be turned into furniture. The company used chainsaws to convert the smaller branches to logs for burning in the house wood-stove. And they put all the really small branches through a 'chipper' and converted them to bags of stuff that now keeps the weeds off the paths in my vegetable garden. Finally, they had this brilliant machine that 'nibbled' away the tree stump to below ground level. All of these services cost extra but I happily paid for them when the nice chap that ran the business came to see me and explained what their 'product range' was, as he called it so impressively.

After the job was completed, the chap came back to see if I was satisfied with the job that had been done. Which I was. He went on to suggest to me that the spot where the tree had been now looked somewhat bare and had I considered having it landscaped? "What will that all cost?" was my first question. "I've no idea", he said, "but I can recommend another firm that does that kind of work", and he kindly gave me their number. "Free advertising or do you get a commission?" I joked. "Absolutely free", he said, "although they call us quite often when they have trees that need felling".

Well, much to learn from this. I felt that I had certainly received a 'service'. That is to say it wasn't just the tree-felling but the other things that I hadn't really thought about. Such as what to do with the tree once felled. I did ask what the chap did when people didn't want the logs planking. "We offer a full waste disposal service too", he smiled. "Do you burn it or something", I asked. "Oh no", he replied, "we do exactly what we did for you". "What do you mean?", I asked, somewhat surprised. "Well, we sell the planks to a firm in High Wycombe that makes furniture and the small logs to a garage that sells them from their forecourt". "And the chippings?", I asked. "Oh", he said, "a garden centre buys as much of that from us as we can make. And they even give us bags with their name printed on them to collect the chippings. The sawdust goes to a pet-shop for hamster bedding although we don't get paid for that." "Why not?", I asked. "My daughter owns the shop", he grinned.

"So", I said, "people pay for your waste disposal service and then you sell the waste products as well?" "It would be difficult to run a business by just cutting down trees", he smiled. "And I run a business", he added. "Have you been in business long?", I asked. "I took over from my father", he replied. "Taught me all I know". The father was obviously a good teacher!

From this case study it is clear that 'ABC Tree Surgeons' was run as a business. And the business had a clearly defined set of products that they offered to their customers. Essentially a service product business, in terms of tree-felling, but with other products and services that followed on. And they 'added value' to the waste by converting the tree into planks, chippings or logs and sold those too. The latter are all *manufactured* products that came as by-products from the waste. Quite a good business model, don't you think?

In this example, it was the same chainsaws that planked the logs as were used to cut down the tree. And so the business owner had identified an opportunity to extend the services offered *without having to invest in extra equipment.* That's not an uncommon event in starting a business — new opportunities present themselves once you start trading. And smart business owners are always on the look-out for new opportunities.

In contrast to the first case study, 'Spot-On Wedding Planners' offered a service that required no big investment in machines like chainsaws when they started in business. The two partners, Dorothy and Julie, both came from a background of office administration and had eventually got into organising conferences for a pharmaceutical company. However, the big company was taken over by an American firm who felt that conference organisation could be contracted out and both women were offered redundancy. Here's how they started their business:

Over a Friday night 'crisis meeting' involving Dorothy and her husband, it was decided that belts would have to be tightened. Especially if they were still going to be able to provide their only daughter Vicki with the wedding that they had promised, when she married Rob nine months later. But the numbers didn't add up. "We'll have to do most of it ourselves", announced Dorothy, never one to be defeated easily. Dorothy asked Julie if she would like to help her organise the wedding of her daughter and Julie jumped at the chance saying, "It'll be good to keep busy".

On the following Monday the two women met and approached the wedding much in the same way as they would have organised a conference. There were many parallels: hotels, travel arrangements, catering and so on. Suffice it to say, over 250 guests were generally agreed that it was the best wedding they had ever been to. Except Rob's mother, but that's another story. One or two of the guests asked, half-jokingly, if Dorothy and Julie would organise a wedding for their child. One couple asked if she'd organise a Golden Wedding celebration. Both Dorothy and Julie took these compliments and smiled.

The week following the wedding Dorothy felt rather deflated. Her 'little girl' had left home. And being redundant didn't help. Dorothy felt 'on the scrap heap' and didn't like the feeling one bit. She called Julie. "Any thoughts about work?", she enquired. "Still nothing doing", replied Julie. They chatted for a while and wondered about setting up their own conference organising business but then remembered what hassle it had been when they did conferences before.

Three days later one of the wedding guests, Mrs Taylor, called Dorothy and asked again about organising a wedding for their daughter. Dorothy pointed out that they didn't really do that but would think it over. Before putting the phone down, Dorothy cheekily asked what sort of budget Mrs Taylor had in mind. "We'd like something similar to Vicki's wedding", she said. "We've saved for a long time and have a budget of £15,000." It took at least two seconds for Dorothy to telephone Julie. They'd organised Vicki's wedding for £11,789.46 (Dorothy was meticulous about costs) and both agreed that a profit of £3,000 for arranging a wedding would be a useful help.

Three days later they were in the Taylor's lounge. "What would you like us to do?", asked Julie. "Everything", said Mrs Taylor. "Yes, of course", piped up Dorothy, ignoring the glare from Julie. "And can we confirm a budget of £15,000", asked Dorothy. "Yes", stated Mrs Taylor. All of the women ignored the pained look on the face of Mr Taylor. "Then what we will do is to go away and cost out a series of options for you Mrs Taylor. See you in a week." Outside in the car Julie said how amazed she was at what had just happened. "Think of all the things that could go wrong", she pleaded. "Look", said Dorothy, "we can do conference organisation with our eyes shut for 2,000 plus doctors and you know how difficult they are. This is an event for 200 people and we have lots of time to plan it. We can do this. But we have to do it properly."

Well, the case story has a happy ending. Julie's husband was an accountant who advised them about setting up their business. They had his help to draft a business plan and were shocked at what it would cost just to get started. Nevertheless, on the back of that plan, they raised a loan of £8,000 from the bank to set up an office at Dorothy's home in what was previously Vicki's bedroom. They bought mobile phones, a decent computer with an expensive colour printer capable of doing invitations, flyers and so on. And some software that allowed them to do project planning and also travel directions. With some redundancy money left to invest in their business and the cash from the loan they took the bold step of hiring the secretary who had previously worked for them and who, rather luckily, wanted to work part-time. Two years on and the business was a success although the name had changed to 'Spot-On Function Planners' since they had found weddings were only part of what they could offer. When asked what 'Function Planners' actually do, Julie then had a stock answer: "Everything you need".

This case study illustrates how a service product business, in this case wedding planning, can be created by people who have no direct experience of the service. You will have noticed that both of the partners had previous relevant experience that could be applied to medical conferences just as it could to planning weddings. The skill of the women was in organisation and planning. The product that they sold was perhaps not just the planning of the weddings but also peace of mind for their customers.

The way in which the service product is offered (how "professional" people perceive you to be) is a critical factor in this type of business. We would argue that a professional service is critical for any kind of business but there is no denying that for a service product it is absolutely vital. Turning our attention now to businesses that "make" a product, let's look at a third case study:

CASE STUDY: WILLIAMS FINE WOODWORKING

John Williams was a darn good joiner. Everyone said so. But making window frames, and worst of all fixing them on the building site on a freezing January morning, wasn't what he wanted to do for the rest of his life. And Peter Watson didn't deserve the job of foreman at Wilkinsons. Everybody agreed that too. So John thought long and hard about going it alone. His Uncle had done it and he figured that he could too. That Saturday John and his wife had his Uncle over for tea. Uncle Peter was John's Godfather and had always enjoyed a special relationship with him, not having any children of his own. When John asked him about going it alone the old man wanted desperately to give him unfaltering encouragement. But he felt unable to offer anything but the plain truth.

"John", he told him, "you're a darn good joiner. Everyone says so. But the truth is that going on your own is going to be very difficult. Why would people pay you a decent rate for stuff when they can buy mass-produced products at the out of town stores for a cheap price. Today, people ignore quality and look only at price."

John had come to expect unqualified encouragement from his Uncle and so these comments shocked him a bit to say the least. "What's your advice Uncle?", he asked.

The old man thought carefully for what seemed like an age and then answered slowly, "I think you have to stop being a joiner John. You have to think like a businessman and decide which of your skills can earn the most money. Forget making window frames, everyone wants uPVC anyway. Nobody could be bothered to paint your windows every five years no matter how good they look. You can make things in wood — what things can you make that would sell for the most money?" John fell silent and toyed with the piece of cake in front of him. Eventually pushing it to one side he announced, "Cathedrals. I could make a cathedral, or at least the wooden parts that go into one." His wife Elaine moved uneasily on her chair. She loved this man, would follow him to the ends of the earth, but this was starting to make her worried. "Well", she said rather uneasily, "you can't buy those at 'B&Q' can you Uncle Peter?"

The old man started to smile. "Indeed not. Maybe this lad is a businessman after all." Elaine still felt the need to fidget and eventually got up to clear away the tea things. Moving into the front room the two men sat down by the fire and started to talk. And they talked. And talked. And eventually Elaine left them to it and went to bed. Sleep didn't come easily for her but she dropped off hours before they had finished talking.

The next morning Elaine awoke to the snore of her husband asleep beside her. Over breakfast he spilled out all of his ideas along with a good many toast crumbs. Some big enough to butter. Elaine listened patiently throughout. "So you still want to make windows?" she enquired of John. "Yes", he replied, "amongst other things. But what Uncle Peter made me realise was that I can make more or less anything in wood. So why make what everyone else is making? I want to specialise in making windows, and many other things, for the restoration of very old buildings. Cathedrals maybe, but also mediaeval homes that have been bought by the rich and famous. They'll take longer to make but we can charge a premium price for it. I've always been interested in the history of joinery and timber-framed buildings; now's the chance for me to indulge my passion and get people to pay me for doing it. I think it's a winner Elaine." John was smart enough not to hand in his notice straight away. He spent nearly six months doing research in the local library and planning out what he could realistically do on his own.

The answer was not as much as he wanted — he'd need someone to work with him. As the months passed he spent most evenings in the library or on the internet. He figured that if he couldn't compete with the out of town stores then he should look at areas where there was less competition. And eventually decided that why should he operate against competition at all? The hours of internet research had paid off. He felt pretty confident that nobody in the county would compete with him. There were no adverts in Yellow Pages or anywhere on the internet for joiners specialising in the restoration of old buildings. He'd even found an article on the internet from a bishop moaning about not being able to find anyone these days to repair woodwork in churches. And best of all, that bishop lived in his county.

Early in the New Year John handed in his notice. Mike Bradley, the young joiner who had been apprenticed under John was clearly upset to hear that John was leaving and asked bluntly if there were jobs going wherever John was moving to. John smiled and explained he was only moving to his own garage. Mike asked if he could come with him, which saved John the trouble of having to make the approach himself. Wilkinsons weren't too keen though and both John and Mike found themselves booted out before the end of the month. No matter, they got paid off and now had time to set up John's garage as a workshop. Their first visitor was Uncle Peter. "We need to kit this workshop out", said John. "No lad", said the old man, "what you need to do is go see my accountant and set the business up first."

The accountant listened to John as he explained exactly what products he intended to make. And said that, in his view, John's product was "hand-made restorations" and that his focus should be on the hand-made aspect. As the two chatted through what would be required to set up the business it quickly became clear that John's savings would never pay for the machines that he wanted. The accountant advised that his cash was better off in the bank, in order to pay Mike's wage and John's living expenses, until they got on their feet. "Why not advertise your products as being entirely hand-made?", asked the accountant. "But that would take ages", replied John, "maybe three times as long". "No problem", replied the accountant, "if you can charge four times as much". And so was born "Williams Fine Woodworking" with a sign on the van that read, "No machines used in our products, everything hand-made". Three years later John's order book was full. He was a darn good joiner. Everyone said so.

'Jim's Diner' was a funny kind of name for the business, since most people think of sitting down to dine and yet Jim's customers all had to stand up. But at least the awning of the converted trailer kept them dry as they ate, more or less. Located on the lay-by of a busy dual carriageway that led from the motorway to the city, 'Jim's Diner' was a popular stop-off for lorry drivers and passers-by. That was until the service station was built just off the motorway. Takings dropped by 40% on the week that it opened and Jim was beginning to regret the £13,400 investment in his converted trailer. But as the weeks passed by, things gradually picked up and trade returned. One of his old regulars, "Big Wally" was one of the first to reappear. Wally explained that the service station was hopeless since (a) it cost a fortune to eat in the restaurant there, (b) it took ages to get served and (c) "it didn't taste right".

Ned, a mortgage adviser from the city, agreed. He liked the fact that Jim used smoked back bacon, free range eggs and cut slices of real bread from a wholemeal loaf. And he liked the fresh coffee. Since Jim could only afford a small domestic coffee machine it meant that he made it regularly. So it was always fresh. And milk came out of a bottle in Jim's fridge. Not that milk/cream substitute that comes in small plastic things that you can't open without spraying it all over yourself. Big Wally liked the fact that he could phone Jim ten minutes ahead of reaching the lay-by in the knowledge that his breakfast would be waiting for him when he arrived.

Eventually Jim's trade returned to the level it was at before the service station opened. Over the Easter holiday, he sat at home and thought about why that was. He decided that what he offered, his product if you like, was a high quality one. So he made a sign that he put at the lay-by entrance which read:

Jim's Diner
"eats that taste right"
No bookings necessary
(but we are pleased to take
telephone orders)

I What is your business all about?

As a way of trying to define not just 'what' the business does but also 'how' the business does it, many people now include something called a 'Mission Statement' as part of their business plan. Here's what 'Spot-On Function Planners' might use as their mission statement:

> **"It is our mission to offer the best possible function planning service within a client's budget and to ensure that all guests enjoy the event in a way that exceeds expectation"**

This mission statement makes it clear that the service is not simply that of planning functions. It is the quality of the service that is the key factor. We think that mission statements are best used for this type of service product business. They are often less useful for businesses that make products. For those businesses, it is often more effective to have a simple phrase that captures the spirit of the product. For example "Think different" for Apple Computers or "Just do it" for Nike sportswear. These phrases convey a sense of what the customer will do once the product has been purchased rather than just describe the product itself.

2 Every business must sell something

All businesses must sell something, and make a profit, in order to survive. And remember that businesses fail usually for one of only two reasons:

- *the business sold less products than it needed to sell in order to make a profit*

- *customers didn't pay for the products supplied by the business*

Successful businesses always know what their product is and who their customers are — this is covered in the next chapter. Some people don't make a product at all; their product is what they do for other people, some kind of service.

These are the two main forms of business: those that make a product to sell and those whose product is the service that they provide.

A roadside cafe makes and sells products based on economy (cheaper streaky bacon, sliced bread and instant coffee) or quality (smoked back bacon, wholemeal bread and filter coffee) depending on what the customers want. And so market research is important in order to understand **who the customers are and what they want;** this is covered in the next chapter. It's obvious that the same product — a bacon sandwich — can be made from different quality raw materials. And not all customers will like bacon — vegetarians may want a fried egg sandwich. So you may need to also consider if you intend to offer a single **primary product** or a **product range**.

HOMEWORK TIME...

It's absolutely vital to be sure of exactly what your product is before you start to plan out your business. Some people don't like mission statements and feel that the word "mission" sounds a bit odd. But the principle is a good idea, so simply replace that "mission" with "aim" and have a bash: "It is our aim to offer...etc". This is a very valuable exercise and well worth the effort. It's actually harder than it might appear to capture the spirit of your business in one sentence. Give it a go. Next, we'd like you to start writing your business plan. But don't panic — no more than one page. Write down what your proposed product is. Is it a service or a manufactured product? Don't worry about who your customers are or what the competition is yet - we'll take a look at that in the next chapter. Then ask a friend to read the page just once and to explain back to you what they think your product is. If they don't get it right, you'll need to have another bash at what you've written. Don't be afraid to keep returning to this page that describes your product. We want you to be really clear about what you intend to sell. Is it a 'bacon sandwich' or is it a 'sandwich made from dry-cured smoked back bacon'? There's nothing wrong with the former — that's obviously just a lower cost product aimed at a different market. You may sell 100 of the cheap sandwiches and make 50p profit on each one – that's £50 profit altogether. Or you may sell 50 of the more expensive sandwiches and make a £1 profit – and that's £50 profit once again. Not rocket science is it?

Easy sums?   Definitely.   But really important nonetheless. If you can follow this then you'll have no problem with the budgeting sums in Chapter 11.

In the last chapter we considered different types of products and concluded that there are really only two forms of business: those that sell a product they make and those that sell a service that they deliver. Just to test this out one might ask, "Where would a toy shop fit in?" Well, if the toy shop didn't make any of their products then we would say that they are selling a service. Sounds odd maybe? Well, when you think about it, what they provide is a showroom for you to look around and choose a toy from their range. The service that they offer (in addition to providing the showroom) is to select a range of toys (their product range) that they believe offer value for money, are safe for children and of good quality. In other words, you the customer are relying on them to stock a range of products that are 'fit-for-purpose'; *they have done a kind of "quality and value" check for you*. So you may think that the toy is the product but we would remind you that what you are buying is a lot more than that.

Now we mention this here because to make the leap from simply having a product to actually making a sale you must consider not only if there is a market for your product but also by what means you will sell it. Some questions for you to consider here include:

People who don't do market research usually lose money

- Will it be a direct sale in which the customer purchases from you in person? If so, will you be opening a shop or an office (premises) or will you visit customers (car, van or lorry)?

- Will you be making sales via mail order from an advert or via a catalogue?

- Will you sell your product over the internet from your own website?

- Will you sell your product to other businesses who, in turn, sell to the public?

- Will you sell by more than one of these routes?

So clearly, any market research must address a range of issues that all have an impact on the kind of business that you need to create — and, of course, on what you must think about before writing your business plan. Let's look at these issues in more detail.

The most important reason for you to do market research is so that you don't lose money! But market research, when done well, can be invaluable in a number of ways. When done badly, it can be unhelpful, misleading or a recipe for disaster! There is certainly a bewildering range of information on the web: when we did a search using Google for 'market research' it came back with over one million hits in the UK alone! Anyway, let's start with a definition of market research:

"Market research may be defined as the collection and evaluation of information about the marketing and purchasing of a product" And to define why people do market research: ***"Market research is done to reduce risk for the business, to increase sales or to develop products or a product range"*** It's often a bit more complicated than this. For example, an analysis of competitor information or an analysis of how to improve your product might be used alone, or together, to try and improve sales. So, for the purposes of a new business (and in preparing a business plan) we might offer another definition:

"For a new business, market research is done to make sales predictions"

The reason that we list this as the definition to have in mind now is that your business plan must make predictions about income — the cash that sales of your product(s) will generate for the business. In fact, for the financial aspects of your business plan it's really quite simple: will cash income be greater than what cash you pay out in running the business? If not, then the business plan is not viable. And this is where things can often go wrong; people are sometimes too optimistic about product sales and/or fail to include all of the costs that they will incur.

When cash flow into the business does not exceed cash flow out of the business then you have a problem.

Now all of this might seem mind-bogglingly obvious. Yet so many businesses really do fail because of this simple cash flow problem. And this is where market research can help — you need reliable and realistic estimates of sales for your business plan. So let's take a look at how you can do your own market research.

Many companies offer market research services but new businesses can rarely afford their services. Which is a shame, since that's often the time when they need market research the most. But luckily, it is possible to do quite a lot of market research yourself. We'd categorise this into:

(i) information from real people in your target market (**primary research**) and

(ii) information from everywhere else (**secondary or desk research**)

Primary research often involves using questionnaires and talking to a sample of people from the target market group. You'd get the best possible information if you spoke to every person who might buy your product but, for products like bars of chocolate, that might require you to speak to five million people! So what market researchers do is to talk to a representative *sample* of people. Statisticians get hot under the collar about what constitutes the correct sample size (we have a statistician at Business Boffins but he's banned from contributing anything boring). To address this problem, market research is often done in two stages:

Firstly, a sample of the population in Britain might be taken as a whole. That sample might ask a limited number of questions such as (i) age, (ii) sex, (iii) do you eat chocolate and, if so, (iv) how many bars do you buy per week? For a big company a survey like this might include 5,000 people. The information it gives is very helpful in matching what age group buys the most chocolate and whether women buy more than men. So let's pretend that it turned out that only females aged between 15 and 25 bought chocolate. Obviously not true, but let's pretend for a moment. In that case, the second stage of the market research would entail talking to a smaller group of people (maybe 100 to 250) but asking a lot more detailed questions. And guess what? Of course only females aged between 15 and 25 would be interviewed because that would be the chocolate eating portion of the population overall.

With the massive amount of information available from the web nowadays, it is often possible to do that first part of the market research via the internet. Saves a lot of time and money of course. For a new business it often boils down to what the business can afford to do. And this is where secondary research can help because it's comparatively cheap to surf the web for information as compared to interviewing real people.

Secondary, or desk research, involves getting data from other sources, commonly the internet in recent years but also from competitor catalogues and price lists for example, together with other sources such as annual reports (big companies produce these every year). These competitors are hardly likely to answer direct questions about what they are doing but it's often surprising just how much they give away in their annual reports. Perhaps that's not entirely surprising since the annual report of a big company is often aimed at its shareholders who they want to impress. More about that in later chapters; let's take a look at a case study now…

CASE STUDY: MANCHFORD MACHINE MANUFACTURING

Manchford Machine Manufacturing is a partnership between engineers and electronics experts and they set up a business to make a woodworking lathe. The lathe has an electronic device that controls the speed of the motor. This is a good thing since the lathe operator (wood-turner) doesn't have to be bothered about changing pulley belts in order to change the speed that the piece of wood is rotating at (bigger bits of wood need slower speeds for wood-turning). They built prototypes and tested them. And worked out how to build it and what all the materials, labour and other costs would total so they had a good idea of the **unit price**, *ie* what it would cost the business to make **one** lathe.

What they wanted to know next was: how many lathes could they make per month, how much to charge (the sales price) and how many lathes could they sell?

Pricing a product is always difficult. Funnily enough, the error that is most common is to charge too little (prices can easily be reduced but it's much harder to put them up). Market research can really help with this. Manchford Machine Manufacturing (MMM) took a pragmatic approach to their market research and started with secondary research. They bought every woodwork journal at the newsagents and looked at all of the adverts for lathes, making a list of suppliers, products and prices. They bought machine supplier catalogues and added other lathe products and prices to their list.

In only a few hours they had a good piece of market research: a table that showed who the main suppliers of woodworking lathes were in the UK, what their products were and how much they cost. They also had, within that list, the names of the main machine suppliers to whom MMM might sell their lathe for re-sale to the public. But that raised a second issue — what would the price to the public be (the retail price) and what would the price to the machine suppliers be (the wholesale price).

Well the market research showed that lathes ranged from about £150 right up to £3,500. None of the cheaper lathes had electronic speed control (some medium-priced ones offered it as an option) so, in placing their product in the market, they reckoned that their price would be in the £1,500 to £3,000 range. Looking more closely at all of the information that they had collected, what surprised MMM was that most of the lathes did not come with a floor stand — that was sold as an optional extra. Their own lathe had a built in floor stand since the extra weight made the lathe less prone to vibration and tests had shown that reduced vibration made it easier to get a smooth finish when turning something like a bowl from a piece of wood. So the expense of the floor stand enhanced the quality of the product. They did not therefore want to redesign their lathe so they could sell it separately. MMM realised from their market research that:

- there were competitor products on the market

- they were competing in a market that had a comparable price range of around £1,700 to in excess of £3,000 (including the floor stands)

- they may have a product advantage with their built-in floor stand

Overall, they felt that they were getting to grips with the data that they needed.

From this MMM set an initial retail price for their product at £2,250 and considered that the wholesale price would depend upon how many lathes a company bought from them; for planning purposes they set the discount rate at 20% for 10 lathes or less, 25% for 11-20 lathes and 30% for 21 lathes and above but realised that they may have to give a greater discount if a big company ordered a very large number. What they set was a 'floor' price (below which they could not go) as 40% discount. Against the retail sale price of £2,250, even a discount of 40% gave them a profit of £300 per lathe.

Having created a product, and set a price, the next step was to try and predict how many they could sell. MMM found it hard to get details from the internet about how many people in Britain bought lathes. So they looked for woodworking clubs that specialised in wood turning and tried to find membership numbers. They also looked at companies that used lathes to make products from wood. And they looked for independent wood-turners. They looked for professional societies of wood turners. Finally, they took another look at the woodworking journals and checked out circulation figures. All of this secondary research gave useful information but it was very hard to translate that into estimates of lathe sales.

Not being a big business (two partners and two other employees), MMM didn't have unlimited resources for their market research. So they took a bold step and did some primary research. They phoned the editor of woodwork journal with the highest circulation and asked for help. To their surprise, he was more than happy to help and gave them what information he had about sales of lathes and, in particular, how popular lathes were that had electronic speed control. He also gave them contact details for the buyers of some of the leading machine supply companies. Just as helpfully he gave them contact details of some wood-turning clubs in their county. And to their surprise he said he'd like to write an article about their new venture, and their new lathe in particular, when they got their business up and running. *He also added that he'd be pleased to sell them advertising space in due course…*

Armed with this information, MMM felt more confident and arranged with the secretaries of local wood-turning societies to take along their prototype for demonstration.

The evenings that they spent with the local societies that following week yielded lots of useful primary research. They had helpful technical comments about possible modifications to the prototype and very useful feedback about price; it was generally agreed that the retail cost would be more attractive if it could be £1,995 and hence not over the psychological hurdle of £2,000. MMM took all of this on board and went back to their business plan. Overall, the market research data that they collected proved invaluable. It allowed them to make some sensible predictions about sales and to market their lathe with some (but not all) of the suggested modifications. They made a few modifications as well that saved money in order to bring the price down. Finally, it turned out that by offering members of the societies that they visited a 10% discount they opened up a market that they hadn't considered before.

This case study illustrates how market research, from both primary and secondary sources, proved invaluable in setting up the MMM business. MMM continued to use the woodworking societies to help them develop new products after they launched their business.

COLLECTING INFORMATION

It's very important to collect the information that you need. Sounds obvious, but what we mean is that collecting the wrong information is a waste of time and potentially misleading. The information also needs to be collated in some form of table, spreadsheet or database according to the type of data that you collect. What are the types of information that should be collected? Well, it's not a bad idea to split this information into categories — the following categories are not exhaustive but give a reasonable guide:

- **What** product you are selling

- **Who** purchases your product

- **Why** customers will buy your product

- **How** you will sell your product

- **Where** you will sell your product

- **When** you will sell your product

As we've been at pains to point out in the last chapter, knowledge of what you are selling (your product) is vital. But also vital, is knowledge of who else is selling a similar product; often termed "**competitor intelligence**". Collection of these data is usually done by secondary research — reviews of catalogues, adverts and nowadays, internet research. It would be typical to make a list of features about your product (including price) and then compare the features of similar products, from competitors, in an objective way.

Who will buy your product?

Do you know who will purchase your product? For a **"business-to-business"** (**"B2B"**) service or product you may already have a reasonably clear idea of who your customers will be. For a product sold to the public at large, you may well be surprised about who buys similar products. This is the sort of information that is often hard to find through secondary research sources such as internet research. Typically, sampling the public at large through questionnaires can be very useful. But if you engage a company to do this for you, expect to pay several thousand pounds for them to sample a few hundred people. You can do this yourself, but it takes time and effort. It may be easier, quicker and cheaper to do this by phone, entering the questionnaire answers into a spreadsheet on your computer as you get them.

Why customers will buy your product

Once again, the real reasons people buy things are often a surprise. Do people buy a certain brand of clothes just to keep warm or to make a social statement? Do people buy a certain brand of ice cream to eat only on their own? Do people buy a certain type of car because of its fuel economy or because it looks sexy? These types of questions are usually addressed through speaking directly with a sample of potential customers. But beware: people don't always give the full story about why they buy certain products. And this gets particularly tricky when people buy for others. Men often buy perfume for girlfriends because they've seen an advert on the TV and recognise the brand but without knowing how it smells. Reasons for buying certain products are very complex. But that's no reason to avoid finding out what you can about why people buy a product.

How you will sell your product

This market research relates more to researching what your options are so that you can make an informed choice in your business plan. Will you need a shop to sell your product or will you have it delivered? Fish and chips might taste pretty awful if bought by mail order... Is selling your product over the internet an option? Will your product be bought by other companies for them to sell direct to the public through their shop or their mail order catalogue? We suggest that you research all of these options carefully; it's not just a matter of selecting the best single option, quite often a combination provides the best business opportunity.

Where you will sell your product

With the internet option of e-Commerce, it's quite possible that your product could be ordered just as easily in Tokyo or Adelaide as it could be in Hastings. Where you will sell your product has an impact on how you will get it from you to the customer. You may need to research distribution options. Long journeys may require that you research, if appropriate, whether your product will be fresh when it arrives. And don't forget regional differences. Buying habits in the centre of London may vary in comparison to a rural region.

When sales are made

Finally, think carefully about any effect that the time of year may have. The public doesn't tend to buy Christmas crackers in June or fireworks two months after bonfire night (but these could be important times for manufacturers selling to retailers). Just as importantly, are there any times of year when your product might sell more effectively? Can any seasonal changes assist in planning sales of your product?

HOMEWORK TIME...

Over the page, you'll find two templates for doing some market research of your own. One template relates to market research for a product and one relates to customer market research. Have a look at the templates and think how they could be adapted for your own use. And do have a go.

Finding out about your potential customers and what they will buy before you start your business will vastly increase your chance of success.

MARKET RESEARCH TEMPLATE FOR A PRODUCT

Below are typical questions to address in comparing your product to others already on the market. As a minimum for your market research, fill this in for your own product and then **do the same** for competitor products. Much of this can be desk-based secondary research. Note that not *all* questions will relate to every product; a vacuum cleaner might need a handbook but a bacon sandwich would not…

- *Manufacturer*
- *Address of manufacturer*
- *Contact details*
- *Complaints department (Yes/No)*
- *Website (Yes/No)*
- *Website quality (Very Good/Good/Fair/Poor)*
- *Can you buy from the website? (Yes/No)*
- *Product Price*
- *Market size (£'s all sales, if known)*
- *Packaging (Very Good/Good/Fair/Poor)*
- *Advertising impact (Very Good/Good/Fair/Poor)*
- *Advertising coverage (TV/Local paper etc)*
- *Endorsements (famous people etc)*
- *Availability (where can it be bought?)*
- *Availability (off the shelf or not?)*
- *Delivery method (Mail/Courier/etc)*
- *Time on the market (if known)*
- *Date new version due (if known)*
- *Main features of product*
- *Any unique selling point of product*
- *Secondary features of product*
- *Options offered (eg colour or any add-ons)*
- *Product range (Yes/No)*
- *Handbook (if required – Very Good/Good/Fair/Poor)*
- *Fit for purpose (works well etc if known)*
- *Reliability (Very Good/Good/Fair/Poor)*
- *Availability of spares (Very Good/Good/Fair/Poor)*
- *Sales service (Very Good/Good/Fair/Poor)*
- *After sales service (Very Good/Good/Fair/Poor)*

This is by no means exhaustive but gives a flavour of the sort of data that can be collected through market research about products. Adapt to your own use.

By contrast, most of the customer market research data tend to come from direct primary research. Below is a series of questions that might go into developing a basic survey questionnaire. Remember that people will usually wish to remain anonymous in such surveys. Be courteous and always explain that you are not selling anything. You should avoid asking people direct questions that may be regarded as too personal; for example, "How much do you earn?" can easily cause offence. One more tip: when asking people to rank a product try to give 4 or 6 choices. Why? Simple: it stops them opting for the middle option every time.

- *Sex (generally doesn't require asking...)*
- *Age (may be easier to say, 21-30, 31-40 etc)*
- *Business type (if not an individual)*
- *Which county do you live in?*
- *Rural, town or city location?*
- *Do you buy {product category}? (Yes/No)*
- *If so how often? (weekly/monthly etc)*
- *Which product in this category is your favourite?*
- *Why do you prefer it?*
- *What would make you buy another product?*
- *What is the most you would pay for a product in this category? (£ give ranges)*
- *Is price more important than quality?*
- *Where do you purchase the {product category} from?*
- *Is where you buy it important?*
- *Would you consider buying elsewhere?*

Interviewing a random sample of people with even this brief list of questions will tell you lots of important information — including if they buy these products at all. Interviewing people who you know buy this type of product will yield information that will help you to refine your product (either what you offer or the price you offer it at). And a feel for which product is the favourite in a category. But beware of bias in random samples; standing outside a church to interview people may yield different answers compared to standing outside a bookmakers. Not better or worse. Just different.

Do try and collect some primary data from potential customers. These data can really help you tailor your product to what the customer wants to buy... a recipe for business success!

CONCLUSIONS — EVALUATING THE INFORMATION THAT YOU COLLECT

The ultimate aims of doing market research before starting your business are to reduce the risk of failure and hence increase the chance of success. Market research gives a 'snapshot' of information that helps in decision making and is a vital pre-requisite to the business planning process. It's not the same thing as 'marketing research' which is a continuous process that helps monitor your marketing activities.

Ultimately, market research prior to your business planning process will allow you to get as close to the famous 'four Ps of marketing' and hence increase your chance of success. We add a fifth category to the list - people.

- **Product** — offering the right product or service for your market

- **Price** — selling for an amount (i) deemed worth it by your customer and (ii) at which you make a profit

- **Place** — distributing your product or service to where customers can buy it

- **Promotion** — presenting your product in the right way

- **People** — remember that you are always dealing with people

Good market research lets you get 'close' to the customer. It gives you an insight into what products and/or services they want to buy and what they would perceive as a 'fair' price. **It doesn't matter if you think your product or service is worth the price you want to charge — it only matters whether the customer perceives that to be a fair price.** Listening to customers about how they want to but products is also important. Do they want mail order and to choose from a catalogue or a website? Do they want to visit a shop and see the product 'up close' before buying?

If you know what factors influence a customer's buying decision then you can ensure that those factors are covered in any promotional material that you develop. There's little point in just promoting what you think are important messages about your product — you must provide information that the customer wants to know. And all of this comes from market research.

It may seem bewildering when considering what information it would be useful for you to collect before planning your business in detail. Such questions include:

- **Who are your customers?**

- **How many are there?**

- **What potential has this number got to increase?**

- **Why will customers buy your product?**

- **Who are your competitors?**

- **What is it that makes your product different?**

- **How do you compare to your closest competitors?**

It's impossible to offer suggestions about what data to collect without considering the resources that you have available:

- **how much time do you have available?**

- **how much are you able to invest in this?**

To be realistic, any small business with internet access should be prepared to:

- **undertake desk-based research**

- **to spend time in libraries**

- **to check through directories such as "Yellow Pages"**

- **and to look, listen and ask.**

How long it will all take depends upon the resources that you have available as well as the way in which you approach the research; well planned research takes a lot less time than poor research! A sensible starting point is to decide on the amounts of time and money that you can afford — and then stick to that! And don't forget to allocate time for the review of the data that you collect. As a general guide, we think that it would be time well spent if you allocated at least one full week to the collection and analysis of market research data.

In planning a new business venture, we believe that the correct way to move forward is to define your product(s) or service(s), assess if you have a market and then to decide upon what form your business structure will take. There are a number of different legal formats under which it is possible to trade; the main ones are:

- **sole trader**

- **partnership**

- **limited liability partnership**

- **private limited company**

> There are four main forms of business structure – ask your accountant to advise on the best structure for you

Since these different entities are suitable for different circumstances, it is extremely important that you consult a professional adviser about which is best for you. Either your solicitor or your accountant can help you with this and either can arrange for the necessary paperwork to be put in place for you. It isn't unusual for both your solicitor and your accountant to be involved in setting up your business. Let's take a look at these different forms of business structure in more detail:

SOLE TRADER

Quite simply, a sole trader is a person who trades on their own as opposed to being in a partnership or as a member of a company. Sometimes sole traders are referred to as 'self-employed' which simply means that they are responsible for their own employment and the necessary tax returns *etc.* Your local paper will probably have adverts at the back where sole traders advertise their services such as "Gary's Garden Maintenance" or "Henderson's Mobile Hairdressing". But it would be wrong to think that sole traders always work on their own; sole traders can employ others. Nevertheless, many people elect to 'go on their own' as a way of starting in business; of the High Street Banks, around half of HSBC's business customers are sole traders. Becoming a sole trader is certainly the simplest form of business start-up and it's the easiest to get going.

All that is officially required is that you notify HM Revenue & Customs, for tax and National Insurance purposes, of what you are doing. You'll be advised to open a business bank account (to keep things separate from your personal finances) and that account may have just your name on it, "Peter Sandford" or you could trade as "Peter Sandford trading as Sandford Shoe Repairs"; those options would appear on your cheque book *etc.* Although a sole trader could use a personal bank account we advise against it.

In any case, most of the High Street banks offer free business banking for a year or more. And having monthly statements that show all business outgoings and business income makes book-keeping much simpler (we all hate book-keeping but it has to be done).

Perhaps it's because it is so easy to get going that many people start off as sole traders without the appropriate planning. Not a recipe for success! Let's take a look at some of the pros and cons regarding becoming a sole trader.

First off, you are the business owner and the boss! Sounds terribly attractive of course — you'll be totally in charge. But that also means that you'll be totally responsible for all of the paperwork and, should things go wrong, for all debts and liabilities. And, as a sole trader, all of your personal assets would be taken into account should someone be chasing you for money through the courts. This unlimited liability that you have as an individual is perhaps the biggest disadvantage of being a sole trader.

Starting off as a sole trader often requires only a small amount of start-up capital — the cash that you will spend in order to get going. This cash often comes from the sole trader and so that might make things 'tight' to begin with. Nevertheless, any profit that you make belongs to you. On the other hand, limited cash to start with will make expanding the business either difficult or impossible.

One good thing about being a sole trader is that you can make business decisions quicker than any other form of business — just decide and do it! That makes sole traders the most flexible of businesses and this can give an advantage against larger competitors.

However, larger competitors can enjoy advantages over you because they operate at scale — this means that they may buy things cheaper than you since they get a discount for buying in quantity. It's therefore important to look carefully at competitors before deciding to set off as a sole trader.

On the personal side, sole traders often report long hours and sometimes evenings and weekends devoted to paperwork. In addition, sole traders working on their own are unable to earn money whilst on holiday or off sick and so must plan their charges accordingly. Nevertheless, about two thirds of all businesses in the UK are 'one-man-bands'. The most popular sector for one-man-bands is in the construction sector with 'business services' coming a close second; in fact, between them they account for around half of all one-man-bands. The remaining half of the sole traders is primarily composed of some form of service sector business and people such as plumbers, hairdressers and so on.

Finally, it's important to bear in mind that whilst a sole trader keeps all profits from a success, if the business fails then the sole trader will have to cover the costs of that failure from his own money.

PARTNERSHIPS

For a sole trader we saw that one person was responsible for the business and, as a consequence, enjoyed the benefits of all of the profits or, conversely, was wholly responsible for any debts. By contrast, a partnership is where two or more people come together as a business with a view to sharing the profits. In similarity with sole traders, the partners have unlimited liability for the debts of the partnership and if a partnership were to fail, the partners would lose not only any money that they invested in the partnership but would also have to dig into their private money to cover debts. Also note that this liability does not just apply to debts incurred by one partner in the business but by any partner.

Historically, the maximum number of partners that could form a partnership was 20 although this restriction was removed by the Government in December 2002.

The important thing is that there are no set rules as to how a partnership must be structured in terms of how profits are shared between partners. Nor are there set rules as to how long the partnership is to be in existence. What this really means is that there needs to be a written agreement between partners that defines how the partnership will work. In the absence of a written agreement, then profits, losses and assets are divided equally. And the rest of the running is in accordance with the 1890 Partnership Act; how current is that? We view the need for a written agreement as *positive* since there is great flexibility in terms of how the partnership can be structured. Having said that, writing a partnership agreement is something that you should take legal advice on and, in our view, they are best written by your solicitor.

Getting the partnership agreement right is an essential step towards creating a successful partnership. It's a bit like marriage; nobody likes to think about divorce but we all know that it happens. As with business partnerships, sometimes things go wrong. And better that these issues are discussed between potential partnerships, and provisions made in the partnership agreement, before entering into the partnership.

The advantages of a partnership can be quite compelling. For a start, it's good not to have to shoulder all responsibility on your own. In addition, maybe a partner (or partners) could bring skills and experience to the business that you don't have yourself. And whilst it may seem a disadvantage to have to discuss decisions with others, in reality it may well be that better decisions can be reached when the different perspectives of others can be taken into account. But don't enter a partnership if you are going to sulk every time you don't get your own way!

The disadvantages of partnerships include the fact that decision-making is inevitably slower since it's necessary to reach agreement between partners. This can be very tricky when there are just two partners. But perhaps the most common reason for partnerships getting into difficulty is when, to put it politely, partners lose respect for each other. It can quickly become a problem if Partner A takes the same share of profit as Partner B but only does half of the work.

We think that there are some key factors to consider before entering a partnership. For example, sole traders can expand by entering into a partnership with someone else. But is that the best route for expansion? Would it have been better for the sole trader to simply employ the other person? In order to decide on issues such as this, it's useful to consider if the potential partners:

- **respect and trust each other**

- **have similar personal values**

- **have complementary skills**

- **have clearly defined roles**

- **can work as a team**

- **share a common vision for the business**

If you can't say "yes" to all of these points at the outset then it's probably a good idea to think very carefully about whether a partnership is right for the individuals involved. Although in the excitement of starting a business everything might seem very positive, do remember that in running a business conflict can be difficult to avoid and the consequences difficult to manage.

LIMITED LIABILITY PARTNERSHIPS (LLP)

This is a relatively new form of legal entity for a business introduced in April 2001 and relates to a new or existing firm of two or more people. It is like a partnership in that it has no share capital and in that the members are free to agree how to share profits and manage the partnership. Whilst all of our comments about partnerships would still apply, this new form of business vehicle has a key advantage over a normal partnership in that the liability of the members of the LLP are limited in much the same was as for shareholders in a Limited Company (see next section). You'll have spotted that we refer to the people in this form of business vehicle as 'members' — this is the correct term to use and they should not be referred to as partners. This may seem slightly confusing... which is why we've written this book!

To set up an LLP it is necessary to fill in the correct paperwork and lodge those forms at Companies House — see their excellent website at **www.companieshouse.gov.uk.** Once again, we suggest that this is not something to do without professional advice and we would recommend that you see your lawyer or accountant. And, as for ordinary partnerships, although a partnership agreement is not a legal agreement we think that you'd be bonkers to enter into this form of business arrangement without one.

LLPs were designed for professional partnerships (such as lawyers, accountants and others) because some of the professional associations made it difficult for their members to use limited companies. We won't bore you with the thinking behind those restrictions. Normally this business form is only used by large accountancy and law firms (law suits can be expensive when advising major corporations). Currently, relatively small numbers of LLPs have been set up but it is expected that many existing partnerships will convert to LLP status once the associated legal and taxation issues have been thought through.

LLPs are required to supply documents equivalent to those of Limited Companies (see below) including financial statements and personal details of members. What this means in effect is that details of your LLP will be available to the general public. This may not be an issue for you to be concerned over but it is important to know about.

LIMITED COMPANIES

Let's now turn to Limited Companies. In law, a company is an artificial legal person with rights and obligations distinct from those of its members. There are just under two million limited companies in the UK so this is obviously a popular business structure. It's quite a complicated process to set one up though. As always, we advise that this is something for your lawyer and/or your accountant to set up. Nevertheless, we should tell you that you could do it yourself by using the Companies House website (www.companies-house.gov.uk) and they do have helpful staff there to guide you. You will have to pay the registration fees of course, have a name for your company that nobody else is using and have a UK address.

The need for the address in the UK is for a 'registered address' which is where you would keep company documents and to where official correspondence would be received. There are also companies that sell 'off-the-shelf' ready-made companies to you.

In essence, we can view a company as a legal entity in which people can own shares. One person might own all of the company (100% of the shares), two people might own 50% (maybe just one share each) or loads of people might

own loads of shares in different proportions. The point being, that **the company can sell a portion of itself in order to raise money** — often a very valuable thing in starting off. The money paid for shares then belongs to the company — in other words this investment is not a loan that has to be paid back. So, the raising of finance (or start-up capital) is one of the prime reasons to start off as a limited company. The other prime reason is that the shareholders have limited liability to the extent of whatever money they paid for their shares.

An immediate question is, "Why do people buy shares?" The answer is not simple. Firstly, when talking about 'buying and selling shares', most people are referring to those shares that are publicly quoted through the Stock Exchange. These public limited companies, XYZ **PLC** not XYZ **LTD**, have their shares traded on the stock markets and people buy them usually for one of two reasons:

- having shares in a company means that you can potentially get a dividend each year: a payment that represents a share of the company profits proportional to your shareholding in the company

- an investment hoping for a capital gain: shares bought now may go up in value and so the shareholder makes a profit when selling them later... of course, as we all know, the value of shares can go down as well as up!

Things are a little different for the start-up limited company since the shares will be privately held and not traded on the open market. How does this all work? Well, to begin with, it's important to think about what can happen to start-up limited companies as summarised on the next page.

Companies can…

- survive and be sustainable

- do really well and expand

- be sold to another business

- do poorly and go downhill

- do really badly and go bust

In other words, nothing is certain. So why would anyone buy shares in a new company if things can be so uncertain? Simple. Because some start-ups do extremely well such that the value of the shares might go up tenfold or more. And so an investment of £100,000 now becomes worth £1million. Tempting isn't it?

BUYING SHARES IN A NEW COMPANY

Buying and selling shares is all very well if the company is successful and grows in value. Even then, there has to be an agreement amongst shareholders as to what the so-called 'exit strategy' is - a mechanism by which investors can get their money back again after a period of time. And then other questions arise:

- How long will this take?

- Will everyone hold on to their shares until an offer is received above some pre-agreed limit?

- Will everyone hold on to their shares until an initial public offering (IPO) on the stock exchange?

- What happens if one shareholder wants to sell shares but the others do not?

These are the sorts of issue that need to be addressed in the Shareholders' Agreement, a very important document that a company lawyer should draw up.

But not everyone has £100,000 to invest in a new company. Some very wealthy people might be able to buy shares to that value and not care too much if the company goes bust. Lucky them. Generally, however, wealthy people will make a 'spread' of investments across a range of new companies believing that perhaps 40% will go bust, 30% will do OK and 30% will do spectacularly well.

This is all about spreading investment risk across a range of businesses so as to build up a 'portfolio' of shares. One advantage for wealthy people making this kind of investment is that certain forms of tax relief can be obtained on profits — an example of this (in 2007) is the Enterprise Investment Scheme (see Chapter 14). And no, that doesn't mean investing in Star Trek related businesses!

Not all wealthy people do that kind of investing themselves however. Many put money into large funds that are managed by business analysts and other professional financial types. One such form of fund is the Venture Capital Trust (VCT). Other funds can be huge — perhaps hundreds of millions of pounds — and are managed by Venture Capital (VC) companies. But it's unlikely that new companies will attract the interest of VC since they will be 'too small' and 'too early' and hence 'too risky'. So generally, investments in small, new companies come from:

- ***the founders***

- ***family and friends of the founders***

- ***"Business Angels" (more later)***

Now, it's important to note that buying shares means that you own a share of the company. If the company goes bust then you will own a share of nothing. In other words, buying shares is not like a loan — you may put money in but you may get nothing back. We mention this here because if you sell shares to family and friends then make darn sure that they understand that they may do well but, equally, they may not get their money back at all. This isn't being pessimistic. It's being honest.

BUSINESS ANGELS & VENTURE CAPITAL

We cover this in more detail in Chapter 14: Raising finance. At Business Boffins we like Business Angels. They are people who invest in new companies (often very risky ones) and we like new companies. Well, we like any form of new business really. But Business Angels are people who back people like you. Enterprising people. Obviously they will want to see a profit. But without them, new businesses would often struggle even to get started. So three cheers for business angels!

Enough 'sucking-up'. By contrast some critics say that VC people have dorsal fins. A bit like sharks. We think that sort of comment is jolly rude. And you wouldn't catch us saying things like that. But the truth is that VC companies are professional investors. And to work with them then you are playing in the "Premier League". So probably not your first port of call for finance if this is your first ever start-up company. But when you need a few million, those are the people to call upon. Although for now, we think that as a small start-up company you would do best to identify local business angels if you are thinking about raising finance from investors. Your accountant will be a good starting point to locate business angels as will your bank manager. We go into this in more detail later.

HOW ARE LIMITED COMPANIES RUN?

The Directors of the company have the day-to-day responsibility for running a limited company. By the way, a Director of a private limited company must not have been disqualified by a court from acting as a Company Director unless special leave of the court is granted and the person must not be an undischarged bankrupt. You are permitted to have only one Director if you wish. A company must also have a Company Secretary who may not be the same person as the first Director. The Company Secretary is in charge of the company's administration. If you decide to have more than one Director, one of those Directors can also be the Company Secretary.

Directors have general duties to the company for the benefit of shareholders, not themselves. A Director also has a duty of care and skill in his/her performance towards the company. And a Director has statutory duties under the Companies Act 1985 which include duties to file certain forms and documents at Companies House including: accounts; annual returns; notification of appointments and resignations of directors and company secretaries; notification of any allotment of shares; notice of any change in the registered office; notification of any change in the accounting reference date; and certain resolutions passed by the company.

SOME IMPORTANT, BUT SLIGHTLY BORING, COMPANY STUFF

In terms of running the company, a Director may not necessarily be an employee of the company. There is a distinction between a Director as an "Officer" of the company and a Director as an employee of the company. If a Director is a Non-Executive Director, that is, not an employee of the company, he/she may be paid a fee for providing services to the company. The company should provide an agreement to the Non-Executive Director stating clearly that he is not an employee of the company. Alternatively, where the Director is also an employee of the company he may be known as an Executive Director.

Check out the Companies House website (www.companieshouse.gov.uk) for more information but your lawyer will explain the various responsibilities that being a Director of a company brings. Also, note that many accounting and legal firms offer a service whereby they act as your Company Secretary or advise and help you to do it yourself. You do not need any special qualifications to be a Company Director or a Company Secretary of a Limited Company but you do for a "PLC".

OTHER FORMS OF BUSINESS

There are other forms of business structure that we have not detailed here — these include forms used by 'not-for-profit' organisations such as co-operatives and various forms of social enterprise ventures. This book is geared towards starting a sustainable business that sells products or services and so we do not consider them here. The British Bankers' Association has more details about social enterprise structures on their website (www.bba.org.uk) but, as always, your lawyer will be happy to advise.

CHARITIES

Setting up a charity takes quite a lot of effort and you would be advised to get specialist guidance from a solicitor with knowledge of the charitable sector; it certainly falls outside the scope of this book. However, a lot of useful information about charities, and how to start one, can be found at the Charity Commission website (www.charity-commission.gov.uk).

In conclusion, we have seen that there are a number of different legal formats under which it is possible to trade; the main ones are:

- **sole trader**
- **partnership**
- **limited liability partnership**
- **private limited company**

The choice of business structure is very much dependent upon what you intend to do and how you intend to do it. If you wish to set up a mobile gardening service employing one person other than yourself, you could adopt any of the above structures. If you formed a company called, "Green-fingers Gardening Ltd" that might sound pretty professional. And it is kind of cool to put 'Company Director' down on forms that ask for your occupation. But is this really the most appropriate structure for your gardening business? For example:

- Is this the most tax-efficient approach?

- Will the associated paperwork be more trouble than it is worth?

- Do you need to raise cash to start the business or will your savings be adequate?

- Have friends or family offered to 'put money into your business' to get you started?

- Will you be working on your own as your own boss or will you work in partnership with colleagues who have skills that complement your own?

- Do you want the business to 'provide you with a living' or do you intend to build it up and then sell it so that you can retire early?

These are the sorts of questions that are best addressed in a meeting with your accountant and/or lawyer. It may only take an hour. And it may be the best hour you ever spent... so make sure that you do it!

One very important aspect of running a successful business is something called "know-how". In fact, it is know-how that a huge number of small businesses are based on. And, generally speaking, most such businesses ensure that they keep their know-how to themselves. Thinking back to when we had a leaky radiator valve in the office, it was certainly the plumber's know-how that got us out of trouble. But, very sensibly, the plumber didn't call me over to show me how to fix the problem in case it happened again. No, he asked me to make him a cup of tea instead. Quite right too — he was protecting his know-how.

However, know-how doesn't have to be a technical skill such as being a qualified plumber. Know-how can also relate to information about the supply and delivery of a product or service. For example, a book shop owner's know-how lies in knowing what books are likely to be popular and where to get those books from. In a sense, the book shop owner provides a service, based upon that know-how, for you as the customer when you go into the shop. Another example is the travel agent, someone who doesn't directly provide you with a holiday but who can access vast amounts of information in order to find what you want.

Sometimes know-how can be applied to business in ways that you might not imagine. For example, Business Boffins recently worked with a couple of ex-Royal Marine officers, Ben Brabyn and Matt Cooper of "bmycharity.com". They were outstanding. It was pretty clear that their military training had been brought to bear with respect to their business: planning ability, understanding of resource requirements, communication skills and the ability to think on their feet and take decisions were first-class. And so know-how acquired from their days as Commandos translated directly into know-how that was useful in business.

Another example is that of Jo Ward who launched her business, "The Trinket Box" in 2006. Jo discovered that her previous training as a florist allowed her to make jewellery. Sounds a bit far-fetched? Well, it turned out that the very same skills needed to wire flower stems into a bouquet could be used to make bespoke jewellery. Which was just as well — she found herself needing a way of working from home when her husband was injured in a lorry accident. You can read her story in the case study on the next page.

On 22nd February 2005 Jo Ward, 26, took two phone calls that she will never forget. First, the police called to say that her lorry-driver husband Gary had been involved in a serious accident and had been taken to hospital. Next, the hospital called to say that she should get there immediately in order to see him before surgery. Five months pregnant and with toddler Katie in hand, Jo dashed to the hospital. Thankfully, Gary survived eight hours of surgery to repair two broken arms, a crushed right leg, a broken left foot and a head injury. "The next few months became a blur", says Jo, "and then our son Jonathan was born."

Caring for her husband and two small children meant that Jo had no time to go out to work and child care was prohibitively expensive. And so Jo searched for money-making ideas that she could undertake from home. A chance finding on the internet of jewellery, that she could buy and sell, sparked off an idea. "I realised that the jewellery was constructed using the same wiring skills I had learned as a florist", says Jo. "I gambled the next month's food budget on some beads and other components and made my first jewellery." It paid off — friends and family flooded her with orders.

Jo found support from Laura-Jane Franklin, Women's Enterprise Co-ordinator for the East Midlands Development Agency who views Jo's achievement as a regional success story. "It has been a pleasure to support her business and observe her success", says Ms Franklin (who also admits to being a regular client).

Jo now focuses on bespoke wedding jewellery including tiaras that incorporate fresh-water pearls and semi-precious gemstones able to match any bride's colour scheme. Her success was rewarded in 2006 when The Trinket Box was awarded the Nottinghamshire Spirit of Enterprise Award for Innovation. Jo's achievement has been an inspiration to others including those close to home - husband Gary is now doing market research prior to starting his own business venture.

This case study first appeared in "The Independent" in 2007.

If you are planning a business based on a **new idea** then that idea certainly constitutes your "Intellectual Property" or **"IP"** for short. And, as the person who came up with the idea, you obviously feel 'ownership' and also the 'rights' to that idea. That seems like plain common sense. Well... you may *feel* that those rights are automatically yours but unless you take steps to protect your idea (before you tell others) then you may well lose out. With a new invention for example, if you tell others about it before applying for a patent then this may be fatal to any hope of obtaining a patent.

New ideas, or inventions, are not the only forms of IP. Whilst an invention (your product) may have obvious IP, less obvious is the *design* aspect of your product. In addition, how you brand your business and product (your business name, symbol, logo etc — what marks out your trading identity) are also aspects of your IP. And of course things that you write (like this book) represent IP too. You need to know about intellectual property rights so that you can take an informed decision about whether you feel it is worth investing money to protect these assets in your business.

WHAT ARE THE MAIN TYPES OF IP PROTECTION?

(i) A **Patent** gives its owner monopoly rights in his invention to prevent others exploiting it; protection is for a limited period of up to 20 years from the filing date.

(ii) A **Registered trademark** gives its owner a limited monopoly to use a word, a logo (or something similar) to distinguish the owner's goods and services from that of competitors and to prevent others from using the same mark. Used correctly, protection can be forever since it is renewable every 10 years.

(iii) A **Registered design** right protects the outward shape or appearance of industrially-made items that have significant "eye appeal". Protection is limited to 25 years after creation, in renewable five-year blocks.

(iv) **Copyright** arises automatically in original literary, dramatic, musical and artistic works, for example publications, recordings, computer programs and even business plans, customer lists and business letters. Protection limits vary between 25 and 70 years; for things like plays and artistic works it continues for 70 years after the author's death.

We introduce IP issues before business planning since we feel strongly that you need to make an informed decision about what form(s) of protection you already have or may need as part of your planning process. And of course, if you feel that formal IP protection is required then you have to allocate an appropriate budget for that. But to start with, the best form of protection is simply not to talk about things with anyone. Except your solicitor of course, but more of that later.

Realistically, you may not be able to set up your business without talking to other parties; this is especially true if you are thinking of going into business as a partnership or by setting up a limited company. But there are steps that you can take. One such step is to have a document called a **'Confidential Disclosure Agreement' (CDA)** or sometimes a 'non-disclosure agreement' (NDA) that you get the other party to sign before telling them your idea. This document is worded such that the other party agrees not to tell anyone about what you tell them and only to use the information that you give them for a specific purpose. That purpose might be to make an investment decision about your business or to allow them to give you a quotation for manufacturing your product for example. These CDAs really need to be written by solicitors and, typically, a CDA may be one to six pages long.

Please note especially that a CDA is particularly important if you hope to obtain a patent, as failing to keep your invention secret will wreck your chances of getting one. Here's a check-list of things to ensure when you come to discuss your ideas:

- Always have a CDA in place before discussing your ideas with third parties
- Mark all documents as 'Confidential' and for use only in connection with those discussions
- Start any meeting by stating that what you are about to disclose is confidential and cannot be disclosed to others
- Write to them afterwards repeating this point
- Always make detailed notes of meetings as people can have different recollections about what was disclosed and what was said

Don't be afraid to insist on these things!

The best place to start regarding IP rights is your solicitor but they may well refer you to legal specialists such as Patent Attorneys. Although the word 'patent' is the most commonly heard word relating to IP rights, few businesses actually invent something that requires a patent application. Nevertheless, you'll find a huge amount of useful information on the website of the "UK Intellectual Property Office" (**www.ipo.gov.uk**) which used to be known simply as "The Patent Office". Let's start with things that most businesses need to consider:

TRADE MARKS

A trade mark is a 'badge' that distinguishes products as relating to a particular business and can be words, designs, letters, numerals, the shape of goods or packaging, smells, colours or even shapes. When you submit an application to the Trade Marks Registry, the examiner first searches to see if your proposed trade mark is acceptable. If the examiner decides that it is, your trade mark will be published in the trade mark journal and left for a period of three months to see if anyone objects. Note that there are over 40 classes of trade mark registration and it will cost you extra to register in each class apart from the initial application fee. Since registration of a trade mark can be renewed every ten years, a trade mark can last forever. It is usual for an application to be made on your behalf by your solicitor or a Trade Mark Agent; ask your solicitor or visit the website of the Institute of Trade Mark Attorneys at **www.itma.org.uk**.

THE ® AND ™ SYMBOLS

The symbol ® is used to show a **registered** trade mark whilst ™ simply denotes a trade mark and is often used in relation to unregistered trademarks. You don't have to use either but you should use the appropriate symbol whenever possible. It will let people know that you claim rights to the mark and using the ® may help you to recover damages if you have to take legal action for trade mark infringement. Note, it is an offence to falsely represent a trade mark as a registered trade mark through improper use of the ® symbol.

COPYRIGHT

Protection by copyright is automatic and, in the UK, does not need registration. Whenever someone creates a new 'work', be it a written article or a recording or a film, copyright in the work automatically generates. The owner of the **copyright** has the rights to control who can **copy** that material or use it in any other way (for example, perform the play in public). Without such protection, anyone could exploit your material without paying you. And so copyright simply gives you the right to control how other people use your work. As the copyright owner for a business, this translates into what financial return you can achieve from the work.

Whilst it is true that copyright automatically generates, it is important to be able to establish when you created the work. This is helped if your written work is published in a dated newspaper or journal for example. But there are steps that you can take with unpublished work; for example, a work can be lodged under a date stamp with your solicitor or even at your bank. This helps to establish the date of creation should someone claim that they created the work before you did.

THE © SYMBOL

The © symbol is internationally recognised and although its use is not essential to obtain protection in the UK itself, it is recommended to assert your rights and is desirable for overseas protection. The owner should use the symbol and add their name (or business name) and the year of publication.

WHAT IS EXCLUDED FROM COPYRIGHT?

Generally, such things as names and phrases have no copyright and hence, if they need to be protected, trade mark registration should be considered. But your business logo is different — it has copyright as an artistic work but can also be protected as a trade mark. One important thing to remember is that ideas in themselves do not have copyright. This is important since it means that although the written document in which you describe an idea has copyright as a 'work', the 'idea' that you express in the work is not protected. This is why you need a CDA in place when giving technical information in a document to a third party.

DESIGN REGISTRATION

A new design for the shape or appearance of your product for example, may be protected by design registration. Eye appeal is a fundamental requirement for a design to be registered as it applies to aesthetic articles but this does not mean that it cannot also be functional. For example telephone handsets or food containers which are designed to be attractive and yet are essentially functional items. The requirement that for any design to be registered it must be 'new' leads to a danger which also exists with patents: an application can be defeated if a designer has published his design before applying for registration. Applications for design registration are made via the "UK Intellectual Property Office".

It is usual for an application for design registration to be made on your behalf. This is a service often offered by patent agents and your solicitor will be able to recommend one. The life of the design registration starts off at five years from the filing date but can be extended for up to 25 years in five year intervals. Watch out though, the costs are modest to start with but you'll have to pay more for the second five years and bigger amounts after that. But if having that exclusivity is adding to your profits that may be well worthwhile of course.

WHY WORRY ABOUT DESIGN RIGHT REGISTRATION?

Registering a design can be vital when the shape and appearance of a product is linked to the branding and image of a manufacturer; in other words, it can help you to stop competitors pinching your design and hence stop customers thinking that their product is one of yours. In addition to any design right or copyright protection automatically arising, registration gives the owner a true monopoly over the design. You'll have the right to take action against competitors (or anyone else) who infringe your design and to make a claim for damages from them. It brings the exclusive right to make, import, sell or hire out any article to which the design has been applied and you can also license the design to others which can be useful, for example, if you wish to let another business use your design abroad. Design registration is also cheaper to obtain than patent protection and the application procedure is far shorter. If the expected life-time of a product is short, and the product will be simple to produce, the design registration may be worth considering.

Take a deep breath. This is where things can get very expensive. But first, what is a patent? Well strangely enough, a patent is really a deal struck between a government and an inventor. The government agrees to allow the inventor a monopoly to exploit the invention for up to 20 years from the filing date whilst the inventor agrees that the government publishes that patent (the details about the invention) for anyone who is interested to read.

In terms of the public good, this means that anyone will be able to make use of the invention (or to copy and make it) after the twenty-year period. In addition, sharing knowledge contained within published patents (for example, in areas such as medical research) adds to the body of knowledge that may help other researchers.

Funnily enough, patents are not available for ideas. A patent will only be granted when **the idea can be put into practice** (although you can file your initial application before doing that). What patents are available for are things like some kind of industrially-applicable device or process.

Note that whilst the inventor has the right to apply for a patent **if the inventor is employed then, as with most IP rights, the employer will usually have the rights to the patent** (although the inventor's name will normally appear on the patent document). Watch out also because if you commission someone to invent something they will own it, and not you, unless you have a written agreement by the inventor to give over ("assign") those rights to you.

KEY FEATURES OF A PATENT

- Firstly, the invention must be new which simply means that nobody has made it publicly available before (*this stops people pinching the ideas of others*)

- Second, it must involve an **inventive step** which means that the invention would not be **obvious** to another person who had a background relevant to the invention known as a **'person skilled in the art'** (*this stops people trying to claim something obvious as their own invention*)

- Thirdly, the invention must be capable of **industrial application** although that doesn't mean mass production (*which at least stops people wasting the UK IPO people's time with things that could never be made*)

- Finally, the invention must not be a type that is excluded by law, for example, scientific theory and mathematical methods

You need a patent specialist (patent agent) to help you with writing the patent and all related matters. But things get expensive; typically, to patent an invention in the major countries around the world over the 20 year patent life can cost £200,000.

PATENT APPLICATION PROCESS

You really should get a patent agent to draft out your patent documentation since it can be complicated and if your initial application is poorly written it may limit what claims you will be allowed to make regarding your invention. Skilled patent agents are able to draft the wording to give you the widest possible scope for your invention. Your solicitor will undoubtedly be able to recommend a patent agent who is skilled in the field of your invention. Don't forget that those who are the best may well be the most expensive. But it's important to invest in your application at this early stage since others may challenge your patent in court later ('patent busters') and they will use the best legal brains that they can afford to do so.

To start with, the UK patent process costs you very little in application fees (but you'll need to pay your legal team). The initial application is free and contains your patent request, your name and address together with a description of your invention. This initial application gives you a 12-month breathing space by the end of which you must submit details of the 'technical claims' that define your invention and the areas you wish to protect. Most people use this 12-month period to do research or to make prototypes *etc.*

Also during this 12-month period, you pay for a preliminary search which is where the UK IPO examiner checks to see if your invention is new. You'll get a 'search report' for your £130 fee (2007) which will list documents that the examiner feels have a bearing on your invention. If it looks like someone has beaten you to it, you have the option to withdraw then, enabling you to keep your invention secret. In some cases amendments may need to be made.

Otherwise, the patent process moves to the next step of publication. This usually happens within 18 months after the date that you first filed the patent application. At this stage the contents of your application are no longer confidential. Once published, you have to pay a £70 (2007) examination fee and again if there are problems you may be able to amend your patent application. Once the objections of the examiner, if any, have been met, the patent is granted and published once again. Overall, the process of obtaining a patent is quite slow - it commonly takes between two and four years to obtain a patent. But once granted, the patent will give you a monopoly for a period of up to 20 years from the **filing date** (so long as you keep paying the annual renewal fees which get more expensive as you go on). Practice elsewhere can differ: in the USA, for example, patent monopoly is from the **date of invention**, not the date of filing. This brings us onto another point - you will need to file patents in those parts of the world where you wish to have a monopoly and, once again, this is something that your patent agent can advise you on and also organise on your behalf.

CONCLUSIONS

Generally speaking, all businesses have some form of intellectual property. The trick is in knowing what types of intellectual property exist within your business, making sure you own what you think you own and being able to make an informed decision about whether it makes business sense to invest money in protecting your intellectual property.

Your accountant will advise on financial implications of IP protection and the relevance to your business. But your solicitor will give a valuable perspective on what is possible and sensible too. Plus your solicitor will advise on suitable specialist legal services that you might require.

Perhaps this chapter has been a bit heavy going (sorry!) since it deals with legal stuff and things that you may feel are of little relevance to your business. Nevertheless, we want to help you "avoid the avoidable" and so we want you to be able to make an *informed* decision as to the relevance of IP protection for your business. Anyway, here are the key facts for you to review:

> Don't forget that a registered company name and also a website domain name are both forms of intellectual property owned by your business

- **All businesses have intellectual property.**

- a **Patent** gives its owner exclusivity to prevent others from exploiting his invention; protection is for a limited period of up to 20 years from the filing date. To qualify, an invention must be new, not obvious to others in the field, appropriate for industrial application and patentable subject matter. A UK application is for the UK; separate applications need to be made for other countries. The patent process can be expensive.

- a **Registered trademark** gives its owner a limited monopoly to use a word, a logo (or something similar) to distinguish its goods and services from that of competitors and to prevent others from using the same mark. Used correctly, protection can be forever since it is renewable every 10 years.

- a **Registered design right** may be obtained in the shape or appearance of industrially manufactured items, which have significant 'eye appeal'. Protection is limited to 25 years after creation, in renewable 5 year blocks.

- **Copyright** applies to things like publications and recordings and even business plans and documents. Protection limits vary between 25 and 70 years; for things like plays and artistic works it continues for 70 years after the author's death.

- ***Always seek professional advice from your solicitor or patent agent.***

One of the keys to survival in business is the ability to get the right help when you need it. And so a list of support sources — including contact details for professional advisers — ought to form

an appendix to every business plan. But it never does. Worryingly, owner-managers often rely on Google when they are in a fix and need quick answers. Now, don't get me wrong, I love Google. But a search using 'business advice' generates millions of hits… a lot of reading! So let's make this simple. There are just two categories of support that you need: help from people who understand business and help from people who understand what you sell.

Top of the list of those that understand the rules about business are accountants and solicitors. You need one of each — add to shopping basket. They can answer questions

as they arise, help with statutory stuff, such as tax returns, and offer strategic help. The bad thing is that they charge for that advice. So the smart thing is to learn about business, the process of enterprise, yourself. This will help you to know when to consult them and make their advice cost-effective — reading this book is therefore a good investment!

One organisation you should know about is Business Link. This national organisation offers impartial information from their website (**www.businesslink.gov.uk**) and their local advisers (*found from their website by entering your postcode*) can help directly with anything from sourcing premises to finding funds. But also look out for their training events — most are free or heavily subsidised. Attending these events is as much about meeting people in the same situation as you as it is about learning from experts — otherwise known as 'networking'.

Next on the shopping list are membership organisations that provide support for small business. The two to be aware of are the Federation of Small Business (FSB) and the British Chambers of Commerce (BCC). The FSB (**www.fsb.org.uk**) is Britain's biggest business organisation with 185,000 members. It lobbies on behalf of small business and their flagship member benefit is a free 24 hour legal advice line — the largest group legal advice line in the country. Coupled to this is a range of protection and insurance cover that is also free to members.

The BCC (www.chamberonline.co.uk) has more than 100,000 members and offers a broadly similar approach to the FSB. It is well known for its training activities and claims to be the single largest provider of government-funded training. A particular area of expertise is in the export arena: in 2003 alone 500,000 export documents were issued and £225 million worth of business was won through outward trade missions. The 'Export Zone' of their website is a valuable resource for those new to exporting.

Finally, you need support from people who know about what you sell. Keeping up to date with developments in your line of business is vital. And joining a Trade Association is a good way to do that. If you are unsure about the trade associations that are relevant to your business, then visit the Trade Association Forum website (www.taforum.org). Business owners often forget that their suppliers are also good sources of information so get to know them well. But take especial care to get to know your customers — you ignore them at your peril.

DOWN TO BUSINESS

All businesses make use of professional advisers and the most commonly sought advice relates to the law and to accountancy. This chapter not only describes the roles of **Solicitors** and **Accountants** but also draws attention to the types of legal and financial issues that you should be thinking about before starting a business. There can be some overlap between the roles of your business's solicitor and its accountant; for example, both are equally capable of setting up a limited company for you, issuing share certificates and registering the appropriate forms for you at Companies House.

In addition to these advisers, you may wish to seek advice from other professional advisers (for example, an **Independent Financial Adviser** regarding pensions and insurance). And it's important not to forget other sources of professional advice such as that from your Bank Manager. However, it should be stressed that a **bank manager** will typically be tied to products and services provided by their bank and so their advice will not be 'independent' in certain areas.

Perhaps the most commonly quoted piece of advice about how to choose professional advisers is to seek "word of mouth" recommendation. Do you know someone that you trust who is already in business? If so, then ask them who they use as solicitors and accountants. And also ask them questions such as:

- are they satisfied with the service they have received?

- is the adviser easy to get along with and easy to talk to?

- have they always understood the advice that they have received?

- do they consider the adviser's service to have been good value?

Try to ask as many people in business as you know the same questions and take a balanced view. It may well be that all of your answers suggest different advisers! Don't panic — this simply means that the professional advisers in your area are all doing a good job! So if there are many recommendations to choose from, simply make an appointment to see several in turn — try and do this on the same day so comparisons are easier.

Of course it's comparatively straightforward to look in "Yellow Pages" for advisers in your area. Many will quote a website that usually contains a description of the sort of services that they offer together with profiles of the advisers individually. Personal profiles on websites usually list the qualifications of the people so you don't have to ask the awkward question directly about whether they are fully qualified and members of a professional regulatory body. Another, increasingly common, approach is that websites either carry a 'Contact Us' feature or at least give a mailing address. Either way, it can save a lot of time if you contact the professional adviser firms and ask for their brochure together with information about the small business services that they offer.

It's also a good idea to ask in your letter or email about their fee structure (coded language for, "what will they charge you?"). Although this is undoubtedly useful, treat this exercise as a way of narrowing down choice to a 'short-list' rather than to identify your adviser of choice.

At the end of the day, you'll be sharing some very private information with the adviser — your sense of trust and how easy they are to understand will be very important. What you are looking for is someone that will help you achieve your business goals (and hence, to some extent, your personal goals) which argues for a long-term relationship. With those general comments out of the way, let's take a look at the roles of the different professional advisers starting with lawyers.

YOUR LEGAL ADVISER: THE LAWYER

Whilst these terms are generally used to mean the same thing, a lawyer is really someone who is a member of the legal profession, either a solicitor or a barrister. A barrister is a person who is instructed by a solicitor to handle court proceedings on behalf of a client and is never approached or 'briefed' directly by the client. Hence you will be dealing with a *solicitor*. So, now that we know the *term* for the person you will be dealing with at least, let's take a look at just some of the areas of advice that you need to be aware of:

- business structure (partnerships and limited companies etc)
- intellectual property (business names, patents, trade marks etc)
- domain name registration for websites
- employment law and employee rights
- health and safety
- buildings and premises
- insurance
- fair trading, provision of services and goods, competition law *etc*

- keeping information about people (employees, customers etc)
- licences — does your business need one to trade? (eg hotel or guesthouse)
- contracts (eg with suppliers or customers)
- the environment (eg waste disposal issues)

This list is by no means exhaustive and, according to what sort of business you plan to run, you may be affected by several, all or even more issues than those listed above.

With respect to starting up a business, in order for the solicitor to advise you correctly he or she will need to be briefed by you as to what you intend to do. Clearly, if you have already prepared a business plan then that is an excellent document to give to a solicitor in order to make clear exactly what you will be doing. But if you haven't prepared that document then preparing a couple of pages outlining your business proposal would be a good start. In the absence of that, then most solicitors are pleased to offer a free initial consultation at which you can briefly outline your proposal. The solicitor will then perhaps offer general advice and may well ask for sight of your business plan when you have prepared it.

THE ACCOUNTANT

Many people have an image of accountants as rather dull people interested only in numbers. How wrong is that?! Accountants are often extremely clever people who can not only advise you on how to set up your business but can help with setting it up in a way that will give it a better chance of success. And they love helping with business plans... which is no doubt welcome news.

Obviously much of the accountant's role in your new business will relate to taxation, national insurance, VAT registration and making appropriate official returns. Nevertheless, it is vital that you do not simply turn to your accountant *after* a period of trading in order to sort things out. It's much, much more useful to seek their advice *before* a period of trading so that you organise your activities according to their recommendations.

It is true to say that many people set off in business in a way that is not ideal simply because they didn't spend a couple of hours with an accountant first. And that can lead to trouble — avoidable trouble at that! Simple things like getting fined by HM Revenue & Customs for not letting them know that you are trading within a certain period of time (*a problem*). And more difficult matters such as setting off in business without really understanding what everything is going to cost and hence not charging enough for your product or service (*a big problem*).

Whilst accountancy certainly involves a lot of number-crunching and financial figures, the role of a qualified accountant is very diverse and, quite often, people-orientated. Advising on how people set up a business through to the strategic management of multi-million pound deals cannot be dull! The sort of accountant that you will require when you set up a business will be a person who concentrates on personal finance issues as well as small to medium sized businesses (SMEs). The simple reason for this is that big companies tend to employ their own accountants.

There are several types of accountant that you may find if you look through "Yellow Pages"; for example **chartered accountants** and **certified accountants**. Both of these types of accountant are usually certified auditors (*which relates mainly to limited companies*). Whatever you do, we would advise that you engage the services of a qualified accountant who is a member of a professional body.

There are quite a number of regulatory bodies relating to finance and accountancy but here are two examples that we think you will find helpful:

- The Institute of Chartered Accountants of England and Wales (ICAEW); go to **www.icaew.co.uk**

- The Association of Chartered Certified Accountants (ACCA); go to **www.acca.org.uk**

These bodies keep lists of member firms and will identify a local member firm for you, either direct from their website or via the telephone if you call them.

Although we show you how to prepare a business plan later in this book, there is no doubt that you will benefit from having that plan reviewed by an accountant before you start in business. Our business plan template offers *one* way of preparing a business plan according to *your* own ideas. Each business is unique and so your accountant will be able to advise on many issues that will enhance your plan and hence give you a better chance of success.

Part of your business plan will be dedicated to a budget termed a **cash flow forecast** — how much money you think will **come into** (*earnings and/or investment & loans*) and also **go out of** (*your costs*) your business in the first year.

The cash flow forecast is where an accountant can really help refine your plan. So, in the following list of things that we'd expect you to seek advice from your accountant about, not surprisingly this topic is top of the list:

- business plan (and especially cash flow forecast) review
- financially appropriate business structure (eg should a spouse be a business partner or an employee?)
- sources of funding — your savings, investment, loans and grants
- equipment — purchase or lease?
- premises — purchase or rental?
- registration for tax, national insurance and calculation of payroll
- registration for VAT and calculation of quarterly VAT returns
- annual returns to HM Revenue & Customs etc from your business
- your personal annual tax returns

But these forms of specific accounting advice are only one form of advice — technical advice. Perhaps just as important is advice relating to who else you either *should* talk to or *may wish* to talk to. Accountants often have excellent working relationships with certain bank managers based upon mutual respect for each other's professional capabilities. What this means is that a certain bank manager may be more inclined to offer you a bank loan if a respected accountant has helped in the preparation of the business plan. Bank managers don't like surprises and so the knowledge that a qualified accountant has advised you regarding your business plan will give the bank manager a warm feeling about whether you have thought things through carefully. Additionally, your accountant will advise about matters such as pensions and insurance and will often refer you to independent financial advisers capable of putting together competitive packages. Also, an accountant will almost certainly be able to recommend business angels (wealthy investors) that you should talk to if you are looking to raise finance through an investment in your business. And, in that situation, the accountant can help you determine a potential valuation for your proposed business — this is vital in knowing how to set a price for shares if your business is going to be a limited company. Finally, the accountant can advise about *how much* investment to seek (not always as simple as you might think).

Many people take the view that they will pay for accounting services as they need them. Seems logical but, and it's a big but, if you do not know what you need it's quite a risky approach. Far better to make a good allowance in your business plan for accountant's fees in that vital first year. And that might also include something not listed on the last page: sitting down with your accountant on a regular basis to discuss how things are going. At the very least, we would suggest that you do this after six month's trading and again before the end of your first year. But what will all of this cost?

PROFESSIONAL ADVISER FEES

Whilst it is important to know what professional advisers will charge it's equally important to know how they will charge. Let's explain that a bit more. Firstly, most professional advisers charge you by the hour and let's say that the fee is £100 per hour. This may seem quite a lot, but remember that if one hour with your accountant, for example, saves you hundreds of pounds of tax then it's obviously money well spent. The key to keeping fees down is to always provide the professional adviser with clear information — if your accounting records are in a mess then you'll end up paying your accountant to sort out that mess before she gets onto the advice bit! And always approach a professional adviser with a clear list of questions. And write down their answers — it obviously costs more if she has to repeat the advice because you forgot what she said. Secondly, how will you pay? Most professional advisers are happy to send you a bill for their time that you pay every month. But, since they are keen (as should you be) to develop a long-term relationship with you they may offer other payment options. For example, many professional advisers offer a monthly set fee scheme based upon their experience of what work is required — this can be very helpful in your first year.

OTHER PROFESSIONAL ADVISERS

Any search through the web, or even flicking through "Yellow Pages", will illustrate what a bewildering array of professional advice it is possible to seek. Although we have listed the solicitor and the accountant as the two advisers that we believe you must have, there are others that can be of help according to the type of business that you set up.

For a business in which intellectual property represents an important component, it is essential that you ask your solicitor to recommend an appropriate **Patent Agent**. All new businesses will have to address issues about insurance and also about pensions and so ask your accountant to recommend an **Independent Financial Adviser**. The advantage of *independent advisers* is that they are free to recommend insurance and pension products from a range of suppliers rather than being restricted to a single company. This means that they are more likely to recommend the product that is *right* for your business. Recruiting the right staff can be a difficult issue and one that can be very time consuming. **Recruitment Consultants** (sometimes called "head-hunters") can advise on a wide range of connected issues from how to write your advert and where to place it through to what salaries will be expected for specific roles. In addition, they can help with the interview process and perhaps do the initial interviews presenting you with a short-list. In all of this it will be necessary to balance their fees against what time you will save and the increased chance of finding the right person for your business.

Human Resource advisers usually offer a range of other services, as well as recruitment, including advising on employment issues, helping to resolve disputes and advising on the tricky issue of having to make someone redundant. Running a business means that you need to know about how the appropriate health and safety regulations apply to you. Your solicitor can advise on this but you may need to ask help from a **Health and Safety** adviser who has expertise relevant to your type of business.

They may also be able to provide appropriate training for you and your staff. For example, health and safety issues will vary widely between an engineering firm and a guest-house.

Your business plan must allow for you having to pay for a range of specialist advice, particularly in your first year, as you set the business up. We suggest that you get your solicitor and accountant to recommend the forms of additional specialist advice that your business will require. Not all of that advice will have to be paid for — some may be available freely through the wide range of initiatives that are funded by government. On that note, one really good government website is that of the Health and Safety Executive (**www.hse.gov.uk**) which contains loads of clear, common-sense help regarding an area many people feel nervous about.

All businesses must sell a product or a service. Similarly, all must make a profit if they are to be sustainable. And that profit becomes liable for taxation. No doubt about it, there's no escaping having to pay tax. And why should there be if we want to live in a decent society? None of us like paying tax but it's only fair to warn you that not paying the taxman what you owe carries severe penalties. At Business Boffins we think that's fair because businesses that do well because they cheat the taxman are cheating all of us.

> Every business needs to make a profit but then becomes liable for tax

But what we also don't like is paying more tax than you need to do. That doesn't mean cheating, it means being aware of how to structure and operate your business in the most tax efficient way. And that's where your accountant comes in. As always, we recommend that you must consult your professional adviser about such issues. But knowing what to ask your professional adviser is made much easier if you understand the basics about how things work.

TAXATION AND NATIONAL INSURANCE (NI)

The mechanism by which you will pay tax and NI will depend upon the form of business structure that you have adopted:

- **sole trader** — working on your own but possibly employing other people

- **partnership** — two or more people working together as partners

- **limited liability partnership** — still a partnership but in which the members have limited liability for the debts of the partnership

- **private limited company** — which can be one or more people who are always employees of the company

What is the best structure for *your* business is very much down to what your business does and what your accountant advises. But whichever form of structure you choose, there will be certain forms of taxation (of the employee and often the business itself) and national insurance (paid by both employee and employer) that will apply by law.

The ways in which these forms of taxation apply will vary according to:

- the business structure (*eg* companies are taxed differently from partnerships)

- the amount paid as salary to employees (*ie* employees pay proportionally more tax as they earn more)

- the profits made over the year (*ie* bigger profit, bigger tax)

- tax rates in force for that financial year (April 6th of one year to April 5th of the following year)

HM Revenue & Customs (HMRC) is the government agency responsible for all of this. Not surprisingly, the taxman wants to make it easy for you to pay your tax and national insurance (see **www.hmrc.gov.uk**). You can certainly deal directly with the taxman (they encourage forms to be submitted via the internet) but our advice, as always, is to have your accountant deal with the taxman on your behalf. Let's look at what this all means in practical terms with respect to tax and national insurance for the various business structures.

SOLE TRADER

A sole trader is essentially one person who owns and operates a business. Many people start off in business as a sole trader. In law, the person and the business are thought of as the same entity which means that should the business get into financial trouble then the debts of the business must be paid for by the owner out of their personal assets (either personal cash or, in the worst case, they may have to sell their home for example). This is known as **unlimited liability** since the *person* is liable for all debts of the *business*. Conversely, as the business and the person are thought of as the same thing then profits made by the business get taxed as personal income for the owner. Hence the sole trader must pay income tax on profits from the business. In addition, the sole trader must pay National Insurance (NI) contributions. The HMRC National Insurance contribution office will deal with your NI contributions and you must tell them when you start trading. You can apply to your local tax office for a booklet about starting your own business that has the necessary form for you to fill in and return to them. We suggest that you do this via your accountant.

When you start trading you will need to keep accurate records of all transactions relating to your business and, in particular, you must record carefully any expenses that could be classed as 'private' or 'business', for example use of a car.

Your accountant will advise you about how much you can earn from your business as a sole trader before you need to pay tax and what levels of income are required to trigger payments of 'Class 2' and 'Class 4' national insurance. Planning expected income, as part of your business planning process, will allow you and your accountant to estimate what tax and NI liabilities you are likely to have during your first year of trading. In addition, your accountant will be able to advise you about when those liabilities will become payable. In contrast to limited companies (see later), your annual accounts (and hence tax returns) are a private matter between you, your accountant and HMRC. If this all sounds daunting don't worry, your accountant will handle any tricky 'sums' on your behalf —

but remember that his fees will be cheaper if you keep clear and accurate records.

If you have employees, many accountants offer a "payroll" service where they calculate monthly tax and national insurance to be paid by the employee together with the employer's national insurance contribution (known as "Pay As You Earn" or "PAYE"). Accounting firms charge for this on a "per person, per month" basis and fees are surprisingly low — especially given the huge amount of time it will save you as an employer. They prepare monthly payslips for all employees and provide the business with a summary sheet that shows the total amount of tax and national insurance that needs to be sent off to HMRC (usually by the 19th of the following month).

PARTNERSHIPS

In a partnership, two or more persons come together to trade with a view to sharing profits. However, profit-sharing may not be equal and how profits are to be shared is usually defined in a "partnership agreement" before trading commences.

This means, for example, in a partnership of three people in which one person has twenty years of seniority it may be agreed that they will receive a bigger portion of the profits in consideration of their value to the partnership. In the absence of a partnership agreement to the contrary, all profits are shared equally between partners. Partners are therefore assessed individually for tax based upon their share of profits from the partnership whether or not the profits are drawn from the business. In addition, national insurance contributions may be different between partners according to whether their income, if different, reaches certain thresholds.

Whilst profits are shared equally or unequally by prior agreement, the debts of the partnership are the responsibility of the partners personally. This is essentially similar to the unlimited liability of a sole trader except that the risk is shared between two or more partners. However, in 2001 an additional business structure called **Limited Liability Partnerships (LLP)** was introduced.

LIMITED LIABILITY PARTNERSHIP (LLP)

People who come together to form a Limited Liability Partnership as their business structure are known as members rather than partners. Whereas all partners in a partnership have unlimited liability with respect to debts of the partnership and the actions of their fellow partners, in the LLP this liability is limited to the capital (monetary value) put into the LLP by the members subject to certain exceptions. One drawback to this limited liability is that the LLP and its members must be registered at Companies House and that the LLP must send in an annual financial statement which includes the name of the highest paid member and their profit share. However, the agreement between members remains a private document and does not have to be submitted to Companies House and put on public record.

According to the profit distribution, as agreed in the Members' Agreement, members will be taxed on their share of the LLP profits in much the same way as partners in a partnership are taxed.

Limited Companies offer, as the name suggests, limited liability for the shareholders of the company according to the capital that they invested. As all companies must have one director, and since a director is classed as an employee, all companies must operate a PAYE system as previously described. All employees will be required to pay income tax and Class 1 national insurance on any salary and bonus under PAYE. In addition, once all business expenses of the company (including salaries) have been paid for by the company at the end of the year, any profit left will be subject to **corporation tax** which is a tax on the company itself. This is because the law views the company as a 'person' liable to tax on income. The amount of corporation tax payable depends on the profit made since different taxation levels apply according to profit levels. An obvious question arises here — should the Directors of a company arrange for no profit at the end of the year (perhaps by paying bigger salaries or bonuses) or leave a profit in the company available (after corporation tax) for investment in the company's activities in the following financial year? This question is made more complicated by the fact that shareholders in the company may expect, or require, a **dividend** to be paid by the company; a share of the company profits according to the numbers of shares held in the company. These can only be paid when the company has made a profit. In that situation, shareholders receive a portion of the company's profit but must pay tax on the dividend that they receive.

So, individuals' taxation will be applied differently according to how money is taken out of the company by employees or shareholders. As well as this, a balance has to be applied as to what money should be left in the company at the end of the year (even though it may attract corporation tax), so that dividends could be paid or for investment in the company's activities in the following year. And you wondered why most companies get a Finance Director (usually a qualified accountant) sooner or later! As you can see, the tax affairs of a company, its employees and its shareholders can be very complicated and require careful tax planning.

Setting up a company may well be the best business structure for your proposed business idea, especially if you need to raise substantial funds. However, the complex financial issues surrounding a limited company need to be addressed *before* it starts trading which is why we are so keen that people write a business plan. Finally, since all companies are required to submit their accounts at the end of their financial year (*well, actually some time after that*) the external accountant can take on a special role called that of an auditor in the preparation of those accounts. This is essentially like an independent person checking your company. All financial records and activities are inspected to ensure that the accounts represent a true and accurate position.

It's important to note that your accountant can be your auditor although big companies may use different firms of accountants for *accounting advice* and the *audit function*. Whatever route is chosen, the audit function is an important process and adequate time must be dedicated to the audit team (often more than one person) when they inspect your records, ask to see original invoices *etc.* We mention that here because, in terms of planning, you must allow adequate time to assist the auditors with whatever they need. But the taxman recognises the demands on company time that an audit imposes and so small companies do not have to go through the process either at all (exempt) or to the same extent (reduced) since the accounts required from them may be less onerous. And that is genuinely helpful for a small company. But remember that every company must submit some form of financial statement every year to Companies House, whether audited or not. If they don't they can be penalised and the directors fined.

VALUE ADDED TAX (VAT)

VAT is a slightly unusual form of tax in that the business collects it on behalf of HMRC. It is basically a tax on the sale of goods and services. You only have to charge VAT if the sales of your business are above a certain level, or threshold, which is subject to variation according to how the Chancellor sets the budget every year. In the tax year 2007/08, you don't have to charge VAT if your turnover is less than £62,000.

Note that VAT does not apply to all forms of goods and services and so may not apply to your business — it depends on how your product is categorised for VAT:

- **standard-rated supplies** — most goods and services fall into this category; with just a handful of exceptions, VAT is charged at the standard rate (currently 17.5%).

- **zero-rated supplies** — this applies to goods and services which are deemed 'essential', eg food, public transport, young children's clothing *etc*; no VAT is added to the cost of a zero-rated supply.

- **exempt supplies** — this includes services like insurance, finance and certain education and training services; as with a zero-rated supply no VAT is added to the cost of an exempt supply — *the difference is you can still register for VAT and claim back VAT on your purchases against zero-rated supplies but not against exempt supplies.*

Registration for VAT is quite straightforward (see **www.hmrc.gov.uk**) but, as always, we advise that you discuss registration with your accountant and let him take the strain. Most, if not all, of the goods and services that you purchase for your business will include VAT. These are known as VAT *'inputs'*. Assuming you are registered and sell standard-rates goods or services then all your sales will include VAT, too. These are known as VAT *'outputs'*. The difference between your VAT outputs and VAT inputs is what you hand over to, or claim back from, HMRC.

When exactly you make your VAT payments is down to which particular VAT scheme you register for. **Discuss this carefully with your accountant** as this will obviously impact on your cash flow. There are a number of payment options available. The most common is probably quarterly with the first payment due one month after the first three months following registration and then every three months after that. It is possible to pay on a 'cash accounting' basis, when you only pay once you've been paid yourself ie not on the invoices you've raised but not been paid for. The only thing we say is MAKE SURE YOU DO PAY! HMRC has a wide range of enforcement powers including fines, penalties, interest and prosecution. For this reason it is imperative that you **keep clear records** (since the VAT inspector may wish to see them at any time).

Calculating VAT is not too difficult even for those of us not too hot at sums! Whilst we would suggest that you get your accountant to help with the VAT return, you wouldn't want to phone him every time you need to calculate how much VAT you've been charged, or need to charge, for every transaction! This is how we suggest that you do it using two examples of a purchase and a sale:

Purchase of an item at £100 including VAT

Cost including VAT	100.00
VAT = (100/117.5) x 17.5 =	−14.89
ex-VAT cost =	85.11

Sale of an item at £100 plus VAT

ex-VAT sale price	100.00
VAT = 100 x 0.175 =	+17.50
sale price inc VAT =	117.50

Not exactly rocket science, but you'd be amazed as to how many people get into trouble over this quite simple calculation. One tip is to use a calculator that can have a fixed number of decimal places after the decimal point (in this case, always two to reflect the number of pence).

CONCLUSIONS

- Taxation and National Insurance liabilities arise differently according to your business structure, how much profit your business makes and how much money you draw out of the business as a salary.

- It is vitally important that you adopt the correct business structure for your proposed business and that you seek advice from an accountant.

- It is equally important that you seek advice about tax planning for the year in advance and that is especially important for new businesses since those details need to be incorporated into your business plan and cash flow forecast budget.

Nobody thinks that tax, national insurance and VAT are fun topics. With the possible exception of somebody I was at school with who shall remain nameless. And this is especially true since they all usually involve handing money over to the taxman. Nevertheless, it is important to have a clear understanding of the basics even if — as we would suggest — you contract everything out to your accountant to handle. Here, as Lawrence of Arabia might say, are "Seven Pillars of Wisdom":

1. Businesses exist to make profits and profits are subject to taxation (tax and National insurance) either through personal or business taxation.

2. It is essential to take advice from an accountant before you set up your business since different business structures are taxed in different ways and one will be best for you.

3. Sole traders, and their business, are treated as the same thing and so pay *income tax* on all profits.

4. Partnerships are similar but each partner pays tax according to his share of the profits.

5. Limited Liability Partnerships are similar again except that, in exchange for limited liability, financial records must be lodged with, and hence made public at, Companies House.

6. Limited Companies have employees who pay tax and NI via PAYE. Companies also have to pay *corporation tax* on profit. Shareholders of limited companies may draw a share of profits as a dividend; these are taxed differently as investment (not earned) income.

7. Value Added Tax (VAT) must be charged by you if your business finances go over a certain threshold but not all products or services attract VAT. You must keep accurate records of all VAT charged and paid available for inspection by HM Revenue & Customs. A VAT return is usually made every quarter and you must send a cheque (or make a refund claim) for the difference in VAT charged and VAT reclaimable.

Final tip:

Visit www.hmrc.gov.uk for information about tax, NI & VAT and www.businesslink.gov.uk for further helpful information

I know what you are thinking… "How can this chapter possibly be more interesting than the last one?" Anyway, don't panic! We have absolutely no intention of trying to turn you into an accountant. And, in any case, that would be a crazy aspiration for just one chapter. Instead, what we want to convey are some of the general principles of accounting so that (i) when you talk to your accountant you are on the same wavelength and also, (ii) you will be better placed to plan effectively and stay in control of your business.

Now, imagine that you were running a big company called **'Megadosh Ltd'**. And imagine that you were the Managing Director and that you had *responsibility for* the hundreds of people that worked for your company and *responsibility to* the thousands of shareholders who own your company. In that situation, you'd have to know (i) exactly what was happening with your company, (ii) whether your objectives were being met and, (iii) be able to answer any questions from shareholders at an Annual General Meeting. You'd also be very aware that you had certain legal requirements to submit financial reports to Companies House every year. In other words, you'd need to have financial information about the company at your fingertips.

Now whilst Megadosh Ltd may have cash reserves to cover the 'lean' times in business, chances are that your own small business would not. So we believe that your need to have access to financial information about your business is actually more important than if you were running Megadosh Ltd! And we also believe that if you were to apply the *principles* of accounting used by a big company you'd be off to a flying start. But to do that, it's necessary to understand what those fundamental principles are. Here's what we think you need to know:

FINANCIAL MANAGEMENT

All businesses must sell a product or a service (I know we keep repeating that). And all businesses must make a profit to survive (try not to yawn). In order to know, at any given time, if your business is meeting that aim you must be able to understand and to examine business results as measured in financial terms.

There are really two aspects of financial management to be aware of:

- The first is **Financial Accounting** which is concerned with the recording of transactions (sales, purchases *etc*) and preparing reports.

- The second is **Management Accounting** which is more concerned with using historical data to predict future requirements and performance in order to help manage the business as it moves forward.

It is important to recognise that keeping accurate records is an absolute, and usually a legal, requirement for a business. Apart from keeping records you need to prepare reports that will:

- allow you to **control** financial resources

- allow you to **plan** ahead

- allow HM Revenue and Customs to **calculate tax** due

It's easy to see that without accurate records (and easy to understand reports) it's impossible to know who owes money to you and to whom you owe money and when you have to pay. In other words, managing the finances of the business would be impossible. So then, it's a pre-requisite for any business that accurate and up-to-date records are kept of all financial transactions. Without them there can be no financial management.

DO WHAT YOUR ACCOUNTANT TELLS YOU TO DO...

But what do you do with that information? What are these financial reports? Well, there are loads of ways in which financial data may be reported but your accountant will advise on what formats will be most suited to you. For example, if you run a flower shop, keeping records of sales against each type of flower will give you information about what flowers are the most popular. So you'd stock up with plenty of them. Equally, knowing which flowers never generate sales would allow you to drop them from your stock.

Now this may seem obvious to a sole trader who sees what sells and doesn't sell every day. But imagine that you run a slightly larger business in which the person selling the flowers is not the same person that buys them. Unless the seller reports sales figures to the buyer then how will the buyer know what to buy? So then, different elements of your business will generate information that will be useful for other elements of your business. Our example here was the simple one of buying what sells best. But the principle is one of using information that you have. And you can't use that unless you *record* it and then *report* it in a meaningful way.

Well, not surprisingly, over the years accountants have come up with several forms of financial reporting that can apply to any business and that can provide useful information (often called 'the accounts'). But to prepare and use those reports it's important to be aware of the conventions that are used. So let's take a look at those.

THE ACCOUNTS

Before we get into this, just remember that you need these accounts at your fingertips in order to manage your business. But remember also that other parties may be very interested in them as well:

- **suppliers** may want to see them to be reassured as to whether you are financially sound and hence 'good for credit'

- **customers** may want to see your accounts in order to satisfy themselves that you are financially stable and hence able to guarantee supply of your product

- and don't forget the **taxman** wants to see them so that he can work out what tax you will have to pay

The three main forms of accounts that are prepared to give an accurate view of a business's financial position at a given point in time are:

- the **Balance Sheet**

- the **Profit and Loss account** (P&L)

- the **Cash Flow Statement**

Finally, the Cash Flow Forecast (what monies you **estimate** will come in to or go out of your business) is an important report that is included in a business plan at the outset and then redone every year as historic data become available from the three reports listed above.

Now, since all of these reports are based upon a set of accounting conventions it's important to understand those before looking at the reports themselves so we need to define some of the important ones now.

FIXED ASSETS AND CURRENT ASSETS

An asset is something that the business owns. Fixed assets are things that aren't for sale but are used as part of the business's activities in making a profit. For example, it might relate to money spent on plant and machinery or a building. Or perhaps to Research and Development or even an investment elsewhere that is helpful for the business. In order to make some sense of this, fixed assets are usually grouped under one of three headings:

- tangible fixed assets (things you can touch!)

- intangible fixed assets (things like the value of goodwill that comes with a business that you may buy)

- investments (money put into other things outside of your business)

Now, tangible assets don't always hold their value over time. For example a car or a machine wears out as you use it. Hence its value to the business gets less over time — this drop in value over time is called depreciation. Imagine that you buy a machine for £10,000 and that you estimate a re-sale (second hand) value of £5,000 in five years time. So effectively, the value of the machine to your business gets less by £1,000 per year over a five-year period. And so you can include this depreciation in your financial reporting as a book-value — what you estimate the value to be between the time that you buy the item until the time that you sell it (or throw it away). You can even estimate a value on any given day since, if it drops in value by £1,000 per year that's roughly the same as £3 per day (well, OK... its £2.74 but let's not get picky, this stuff is tricky enough anyway).

Fixed assets are one form of asset but there is another form — current assets. And accountants have a lovely definition of a current asset: it's simply anything that isn't a fixed asset. So these would include things that the business owns that have value. An obvious form of current asset therefore is cash in the business account.

Slightly less obvious, but still something of value to the business, is something called 'debtors', which simply means that cash owed to the business by customers who have been supplied with goods or services on credit for example. Another less obvious form of current asset is stock. And this doesn't just include any raw materials that the business has in the warehouse for example. It also includes work-in-progress which relates to products underway but not yet ready for sale. Of course any finished goods (products ready for sale) are also current assets.

Just to be absolutely clear about this, let's think about a fried egg sandwich. The *current asset* of cash was used to buy eggs, bread, butter *etc.* Thus, the egg in the fridge and the loaf of bread are *raw materials*. Whilst the egg is being fried and the slices of bread buttered the items become *work-in-progress*. When the fried egg sandwich is made it becomes *finished goods*. Now if the hungry customer pays immediately then it gets converted back to cash. If, on the other hand, you agree that the hungry customer can pay you the next day, then he becomes a *debtor*. But it's still all about the movement of current assets. And those are always described in financial terms.

By the way, the fried egg sandwich has more value than the raw ingredients since you *added value* during the production process. Which is where you made the *profit*. But only, of course, if you charged enough extra over the costs of the raw materials to cover your other costs such as gas for the fryer, cooking oil, the labour *etc.* Which is all about *pricing*. So there you have it. Business finance explained in a fried egg sandwich. Which at least means this book is suitable for vegetarians. And not as boring as most accounting textbooks.

LIABILITIES

In contrast to assets of the business, liabilities are amounts owed by the business to other parties. The convention is to sort this lot out into one of three categories:

- **Trade Creditors** — this relates to money on account that you owe for something that has been supplied to the business. For example, an invoice that you need to pay in 30 days

- **Other Creditors** — this includes payments that you know you will have to make for tax and VAT to HM Revenue & Customs

- **Sources of Finance** — this might be a bank loan or some other form of debt used to finance the business

Now, most of the above can be reported with an exact amount or a very good estimate. In cases where the estimate cannot be made very reliably, then a *provision* (your best estimate) is made for that in the accounts. Now, it goes without saying that in any set of accounts it is vital to ensure that all assets and liabilities are valued accurately. 'Forgetting' to include a liability or over-inflating the value of an asset isn't unknown. Those that do this kind of thing soon find that their business gets out of control at best.

ASSET AND LIABILITY VALUATION CONCEPTS

There are three main accounting conventions that apply to valuing assets and liabilities:

- **Consistency** — pick a method of valuation and generally stick to it. If you change methods from one year to the next just to make the figures look better, that's cheating; but sometimes accepted practice does change.

- **Prudency** — make sure that valuations are made at the lower end of a range ie don't be over-optimistic.

- **Going concern** — if there is a chance that the business is sinking then you may have to sell off some assets to realise cash. And a 'quick sale' may not realise a sale price that might otherwise be expected. So when faced with that situation the value of the asset has to be reduced to reflect the 'quick sale' value.

In order to make the most sense out of liabilities, it's important to know when the business must pay what it owes to others. Some payments will be due in 30 days, others at 60 or even 90 days whilst some may not be repayable for years. This can be all terribly confusing. Anyway, since accounts are prepared at least once a year, it's important to know at least which creditors will need to be paid within the coming year and which at a time after that. Hence the convention is to group liabilities into those '*falling due within one year*' and '*those due after one year*'. Now, it's not rocket science to figure out that the net assets of a business can be found by simply subtracting the value of all liabilities from the total of all fixed and current assets. Which brings us neatly on to the Balance Sheet.

So not as complicated as you perhaps thought?

BALANCE SHEET

The balance sheet is a financial report that gives a summary of the financial situation of the business at a given point in time. It's like a financial photograph. It shows not only the net assets (all assets minus all liabilities) but also the sources of funds and how those funds are being used. Here's the simplest example for a small company, Minidosh Ltd:

Minidosh Ltd

Balance Sheet as at 30th September 2006

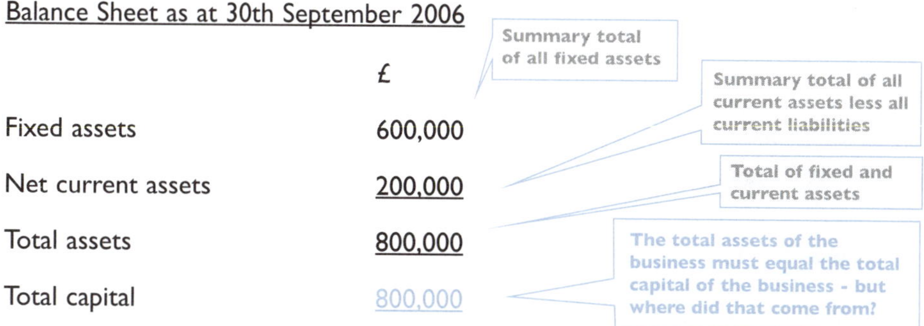

	£
Fixed assets	600,000
Net current assets	200,000
Total assets	800,000
Total capital	800,000

The balance sheet is said to 'balance' because the money used within the business, the capital, is viewed as a liability (as if the business owed that money to whoever put it into the business in the first place). Thus, total assets = total capital. However, it's possible to breakdown the balance sheet a little further as follows:

<u>Balance Sheet as at 30th September 2006</u>

£

	£
Property and machines	600,000
Stock	110,000
Cash	50,000
Debtors and cash	120,000
Current liabilities	(80,000)
Net current assets	200,000
Assets employed	800,000
Loan capital	500,000
Share capital	100,000
Reserves	200,000
Total capital employed	800,000

We can see that fixed assets relate to buildings and machinery (no intangible or investment fixed assets)

Current assets relate to quite a bit of stock (£110,000) plus some cash (£50,000) but with £120,000 owed to the business by customers

The business owes £80,000 (note that negative amounts are put in brackets)

Net current assets simply relates to current assets less current liabilities

We can see that assets employed is the total of fixed assets and net current assets

The capital in the business relates to where funds have come from

The total capital employed identifies a loan of £500,000 together with investment of £100,000 plus reserves

In this extended form of the balance sheet we can see more clearly where the assets are employed and also what the capital relates to; loan, investment *etc.*

PROFIT AND LOSS ACCOUNT (P&L)

Whilst the balance sheet tells us about the sources of capital and how it is dispersed across assets at any moment in time, it tells us little about how profitable the business has been over a certain period (usually one year). Hence another convention used by accountants is to prepare a Profit and Loss account report. There's an example from a small company with two employees, called 'Boffins Widgets Ltd', shown on the next page.

Boffins Widgets Ltd

<u>*Profit and loss account for the*</u>

<u>*12 month period ended 31.12.06*</u>

	£	£
Sales turnover (A)		78,500
Less **cost of goods**		
for goods sold **(B)**		
Opening Stock	5,600	
+ Purchases	19,600	
— Closing Stock	6,300	**18,900**
Gross profit (C=A-B)		**59,600**
Less **operating expenses (D)**		
Salaries	36,300	
Manufacturing	6,550	
Facilities & admin	4,600	
Advertising	1,250	
Distribution	2,150	
Depreciation	1,050	**51,900**
Operating Profit (E=C-D)		7,700
Taxation **(F)**		1,540
Profit after tax (G=E-F)		**6,160**
Dividends **(H)**		2,000
Retained profit (I=G-H)		**4,160**

Now, we can get quite a lot of information from the profit and loss account — more information about trading performance than was possible from the balance sheet. This is because the balance sheet only gives a snapshot of the financial position of the company at any one point in time. From the P&L account example, we can see that, over the accounting period, the business was in profit and that it made enough profit to afford a dividend for shareholders as well as retaining some of that profit within the business for expenditure in the following year.

So from the profit and loss account, Boffins Widgets Ltd looks in good shape. But what if the business owed £75,000 to a supplier? Obviously it would be in trouble — but that is not obvious from the P&L account. It is therefore normal to look at the P&L account for a business in conjunction with the balance sheet. *In that way, it is possible to get a view of profitability performance and the true financial position of the company together.*

The balance sheet shows a snapshot of capital since capital = assets — liabilities. The profit and loss account shows how business activity, over a certain period, has created additional wealth (or otherwise) for the business owners and is therefore a measure of financial performance. **Taken together, these two reports give a good summary of the state of the business.** But there is another (it's the last one… hang in there) financial report that we'd like you to be aware of…

CASH FLOW STATEMENT

Now, just cast your mind back to the bit where we explained how assets and liabilities are valued. We said then that good accounting conventions meant that the business had to recognise financial transactions that hadn't yet happened. Remember? The debtors bit of current assets related to customers that owed the business money. They hadn't paid yet but the balance sheet recognised the fact that they owed money and that the business had a reasonable expectation that they would pay. Hence this was included as a current asset. Likewise, we said that you had to include debts that the business hadn't paid off yet. We also broke that down into liabilities payable within one year and those that fell after one year.

Well cash flow ignores all of that. It's more like a look at the bank statement for the business — what cash has actually gone into the business and what cash has come out of the business. So it's a bit like the profit and loss account in that it measures financial performance over a period but, unlike the P&L, it only includes actual payments in or out of the business. So what types of cash flow are there?

1. **Net cash flow from operating activities**

   Operating activities give rise to both income and expenditure. **Operational Expenditure ("OpEx")** is something that you will need to estimate in the cash flow forecast that must be prepared as part of a business plan. You'll also need to predict what **sales of products or services** the business will achieve. Net cash flow from operating activities can be calculated by subtracting payments to suppliers and employees from receipts from customers.

2. **Costs of borrowing or interest received from investments**

   How much you have to pay as interest on a loan or how much interest you receive from an investment.

3. **Taxation**

   Payments of corporation tax during the accounting period.

4. **Capital Expenditure ("CapEx")**

   Any cash spent on fixed assets.

5. **Financing**

   For example, cash raised from investors or banks and repayment of any loans.

6. **Equity dividends**

   Cash paid out of the business to shareholders (or the owner) as a share of post-tax profit.

When a business is up and running, it's not unusual for a cash flow statement to be put into annual reports alongside those from previous years. The reason for that is to look at financial performance over time. Ideally, a good business will generate positive cash flow which, in turn, can be distributed to shareholders (or the owner). So accountants like to look at cash flow statements and check on how much positive cash flow the business is able to generate from its operating activities.

Looking at the overall cash flow in any one year can be misleading. For example, in one year a business may have an overall negative cash flow, but why was that? It may be because the operating activities failed to yield positive cash flow. Or, it may be because the business made a big Capital Expenditure payment that year — perhaps invested heavily in new equipment. So the overall cash flow that year may have been negative but the increase in fixed asset expenditure could have a significant effect on earnings in future years. Thus looking at the business's ability to generate cash flow from income is, quite often, more important than the overall cash flow in any one period. Hence interpretation of accounting reports requires a little prior knowledge.

SEBASTIAN'S FOOTBALL ACADEMY LTD

Cash Flow Statement for the period ended 30.6.06

	2006	2005
	£000s	£000s
Net cash inflow from operations	280	180
Interest paid	(20)	(20)
Capital expenditure	(160)	(80)
Equity dividends paid	(40)	(20)
Net cash flow	60	60

So from this simple cash flow statement, it can be seen that the net cash flow is positive for each of the two years. In addition, is the financial performance the same each year? Well, if you look at net cash flow it is the same at £60,000 for each of the two years. However, the net cash flow from operations has increased from £180,000 in 2005 to £280,000 in 2006 which reflects a good improvement. And of that net cash inflow, Sebastian wisely invested £80,000 in the business as capital expenditure (fixed assets) in 2005 which may explain the improved net cash flow inwards in 2006. We can surmise that he is similarly investing in the future by investing £160,000 in capital expenditure from the £280,000 net cash inflow from operations in 2006. The overall picture is a business that is growing and that is investing in its future. **So the cash flow statement can tell you about financial performance and management decisions.**

This has been a tough module for those with no prior knowledge. Sorry about that. But we have tried hard to limit information to only those things that we think it would be really sensible for you to be aware of. Balance sheets, profit and loss accounts and cash flow statements are three financial reports that your accountant is likely to generate for your business *whatever the business structure.* We've used examples from limited companies but the principles apply equally to sole traders and partnerships. They are merely a convention. But a good one, since together the reports allow you to understand capital use and financial performance.

Many of the concepts introduced in this chapter will be explained in further detail in later chapters. What we really want you to take away from this chapter is an awareness of the need to understand how capital is used in a business and how financial performance can be measured using standard accounting principles. We also want you to think about cash flow. People say that 'cash flow is king' and we agree. It's no good how wonderful your product is if your overall cash flow ends up being negative.

The business plan will contain a cash flow forecast. Typically this will be for a period of at least one year forwards and sometimes three or five years. That cash flow forecast will be your estimate of how much money the business will need to get started, how much it will cost to run the business every month, how much money you estimate to generate from sales of your product or service and, ultimately, how soon you will be in profit and how big that profit will be.

To help you with that cash flow forecast we would advise strongly that you get the assistance of your accountant. They are really good at it and will point out all sorts of things that you may have forgotten and offer loads of good ideas. But to get the best from your accountant, it helps if you speak their language. So we hope that this chapter will have given you a reasonable introduction to the basics of accounting. If you feel that this has all been a bit heavy going then be aware that **all business owners need to monitor financial performance — it's vital for business success.**

Whilst this chapter cannot address the types of premises or equipment that your business will require (*each business is unique and you'll know better than us what you'll need*) what we aim to do is to inform you about related matters. In addition to looking at opportunities currently available, we'd also like to look at the associated issues of Health & Safety as well as financing.

PREMISES

With the advent of the internet it's now possible to carry out many forms of work from more or less anywhere in the world where you can make a phone connection. But despite these new ways of working, every new business will need a base from which to operate. And you'll probably need a **registered address** – that place where official mail will be delivered to (perhaps invoices, HMRC letters or other official letters). Many new businesses operate from a location that is not their registered address. Instead, they may use the address of their accountant for example - of course this has to be done by arrangement. We can think of five forms of 'premises' that you need to be aware of:

- **working from your home address**

- **an incubator facility**

- **bespoke offices**

- **workshops and warehouses**

- **shops, restaurants and hotels etc**

WORKING FROM YOUR HOME ADDRESS

If your business proposal is to operate as a sole trader providing, for example, a wedding planning service then it's obviously possible for you to do that from home. Perhaps from a spare bedroom converted to an office. And since you'd be working quietly away it's unlikely that you'd offend any of your neighbours. If, on the other hand, you intend to repair cars then it may not be possible to do that at home.

Would the neighbours find your noisy activities appealing? Would they like cars parked all over the place in the daytime? Would those parked cars constitute a hazard for young children playing in your street during the daytime? These sorts of questions all have, generally speaking, an adverse effect on your neighbours. Ask yourself honestly, would you like it? For these reasons, what you intend to do from home may require you to seek **official permission** since you would be seeking a 'change of use' for your home from purely domestic to a mixture of domestic and business purposes. That may also have an effect on the rates that you will be required to pay. In considering whether **planning permission** will be required there are some key questions to address:

- will your home change from being used mainly as a private residence?

- will any part of your home become separated from the dwelling in a way where it becomes unsuitable for residential use?

- will working from home mean lots of visitors?

- will you be doing anything that might be considered unusual for a residential area?

- will any of your business activities disturb your neighbours (eg noise or smells), especially at unreasonable hours?

Your local planning authority will be able to advise you but, if the answer to any of the above questions is 'yes', then you are likely to need planning permission. In addition, if your home is a listed building then other considerations might apply. Certain activities will require other forms of permission, perhaps in the form of a **licence**, and examples might be:

- Childminding (Social Services)

- Animal breeding (Environmental Health)

- Selling food (Food hygiene and Environmental Health)

It will be very important to check about whether using part of your home for business purposes will give rise to a **business rate** being levied. This is very important because the decision makers, **The Valuation Agency**, are part of the HMRC.

Still on the finance side, it may well be that your mortgage lender will need to be notified about the proposed change of use. Also, check that your deeds do not contain a restrictive covenant that forbids you to do things related to your proposed business activity. Many deeds have restrictive covenants that forbid certain things such as mining and pig breeding — perhaps not relevant to you but check what is forbidden. If you rent your property then you will need to seek permission from your landlord if you intend to work from home. Think carefully also about impact upon service providers. Some providers charge a different tariff for business use; for example electricity or the telephone. Whilst on the subject of electricity, would you require three-phase supply (if that means nothing to you then don't worry about it)? Think also about any waste that your business activity might generate and remember that only domestic waste is collected without additional charge. Any additional services for disposal of business waste would need to be discussed with the Council's Environmental Services department. You'll need specialist insurance to work from home (see the next chapter) so ask your accountant about what you will require and then seek advice from an independent financial adviser.

If by now you are beginning to think that working from home isn't as simple as it seems then you are right. However, things are moving forward as more and more people start to work from home such that 'red-tape' is being reduced. The advent of the internet has made home-working possible for many people and some businesses are now encouraging their employees to work from home. Perhaps as many as 5% of the workforce now work from home. And other pressures add to this trend. The benefits of reduced car usage, for environmental reasons, adds further weight to the move towards working from home. All of this change in society means that things are getting easier but you must always get the appropriate permissions.

We suggest that one way of sorting out what you need to do is to get your solicitor to read your business plan and advise you on what forms of permission will be required. We would also advise strongly not to undertake any form of business activity from home until you have taken advice either from your professional adviser or from the relevant local, or national, body; for example your local council. Finally, Health and Safety issues apply at home too; see the later section in this chapter.

INCUBATOR FACILITY

An incubator facility offers a kind of 'easy introduction' to having your own separate business premises. Incubator facilities are becoming increasingly common thanks to both public and private initiatives. In essence, an incubator facility is a business facility that offers rented space to new, or young, businesses under certain favourable terms and usually with certain forms of support. For example the rent charged often includes a portion for:

- business rates

- office cleaning

- access to high-speed internet connection

- a shared receptionist who takes messages and greets visitors at the front door

- access to a 'tea-room' or even a canteen

In addition, the terms of the rental are usually **'easy-in, easy-out'** which means that they make it easy for you to move in quickly and that the notice period (when you decide to move on) is quite short, perhaps only one month as compared to six or 12 months in other forms of rented premises. Other services are usually available and these range from use of a meeting room with audio-visual facilities, catering for meetings and so on; normally you are charged extra for these things. Other, less obvious, benefits from being in an incubator facility generally arise from access to the tea-room. This may sound odd, but asking advice from people who are running their own small business about problems as they arise is a great source of useful help. It also helps to build networks amongst small businesses and you may well find that another small business in an incubator facility offers a service that you need; for example, information technology expertise or website design.

One disadvantage to bear in mind is that incubator facilities are for incubation! In other words, these facilities are designed to help small businesses 'get going' and have an expectation that you will move on once established. Some incubator facilities rent space on the condition that you move out after a couple of years for example. But that's only fair it seems to us. And we hope that your business would grow such that you need to move into bigger premises.

BESPOKE OFFICES AND PREMISES

By this term we mean separate business premises to be occupied by your business on a more permanent basis than an incubator facility. Since you want to have stability for your business it's always important to consider your plans for growth so that you find premises which are not too big but which have extra space that you will grow into over a sensible period of time. And speaking of time, since you want stability for your business it's sensible to negotiate a notice period appropriate for you; this may mean a six, 12, 24 month or even longer notice period. It's certainly possible to rent premises for 10 years if you wish.

Now taking this sort of building is a big step and not one to be undertaken lightly. You must have a very robust business plan and a clear expectation of income before committing to a large rent for a long period of time. For this reason, such steps are usually taken after occupying more modest accommodation in order to 'test the business'. Some businesses fail because they 'grow too fast' without the necessary capital or funding and can mean that they are committed to expensive big buildings for a long lease when more modest facilities might have been more appropriate.

You will need several professional advisers to assist you if you intend to rent this form of business premises. In particular, you will certainly need a solicitor to advise about the contract. You may need a surveyor and/or an architect to advise about conversion of the building for your needs. And you should certainly take advice from your accountant about what form of business premises will be right for you.

WORKSHOPS AND WAREHOUSES

Many of the comments above apply to buildings that will be dedicated to workshops or for warehousing. But for those, specialist advice will be required regarding Health and Safety issues (see next section) as well as many other factors such as site security, insurance, transport, environmental impact and so on. Professional advisers often operate within a local network of other advisers whose work they know and respect. This means that either your solicitor or accountant will probably be able to advise you about what forms of other advice to seek and to whom you might talk to locally.

They may even recommend that you appoint a specialist to oversee the whole project, both identifying suitable premises and handling all negotiations for you. All of this depends on the scale of the project and the type of business that you will be undertaking but, as always, you must get professional advice. And that starts with your accountant and your solicitor.

SHOPS, RESTAURANTS AND HOTELS etc

This category of business premises is slightly different since the building itself is an integral part of the business. What we mean by this is that the location and appearance of the building are an integral part of your selection process and these features may override other considerations. On the one hand, a modern building with excellent parking facilities may be a better business prospect than a 16th Century 'character' building with poor parking for customers. In selecting this type of facility, it is often the case that you may be buying the business rather than simply buying the building. As always, an accountant's advice should be sought as to the past performance of such a business, your trading prospects and a likely valuation. Alternatively, you may buy or rent a building with a view to turning it into a restaurant or a hotel; advice will need to be sort regarding planning permission for change of use as well as the necessary licences that will be required. Your solicitor will be able to advise on these matters.

Shops, restaurants and hotels may be bought, leased or built from scratch. Each route will require that you seek advice from specialist professional advisers such as chartered town planners for example. If in doubt, show your business plan to your accountant and solicitor and seek their advice.

This is not the sort of business that you should enter into on impulse. It will be fraught with problems if you are keen, but your partner is not, particularly where you 'live over the shop' such as in a pub. This chapter isn't concerned with your motives for wanting to acquire a pub or a restaurant but these type of business premises are not for the inexperienced. If you already have the right experience then please skip over the next section.

If you have no experience of running a pub, hotel or restaurant then think very carefully before 'taking the plunge'. For example, could you work in a pub on a part-time basis to get some experience. If you think that running a pub is all about pulling a few pints and chatting with the locals then think again - it's very hard work with very long hours. You will also need some formal training in order get the National Licensee's Certificate (this covers licensing laws and your responsibilities).

You can undertake courses for this qualification via The British Institute of Innkeeping. Check their website at www.bii.org or find further advice about buying catering establishments at www.caterer.com. You can find lots of advice about buying pubs, restaurants or hotels at www.caterer.com including information about the planning process relevant to these forms of planning applications known as 'A3'.

HEALTH AND SAFETY

You will need to be aware of **Health and Safety** issues when you set up in business, even if working from home since Health and Safety (H&S) applies to almost all work activities and almost all businesses, however small. The framework for 'Health and Safety' is set out in the 'Health and Safety at Work Act 1974' which sets out the general duties that employers have towards employees and members of the public. It also sets out what duties employees have to each other and to themselves. Lots of useful information on this area can be found at the government's **'Health and Safety Executive (HSE)'** website **www.hse.gov.uk** which is, incidentally, a very helpful website with many downloadable leaflets that will help you. The key points of H&S are:

- employees must take care of others but also themselves

- employers must protect employees and the general public from harm due to the activities of the business

- suppliers of things that might be dangerous without proper use, such as equipment, machinery or chemicals etc, have to make sure that their products are safe and provide adequate information

And, of course, there are responsibilities for people who design, install or transport potentially dangerous things.

In running a business, the main requirement is that the employer must carry out a risk assessment. This is quite easy for an office environment of course but more complex for potentially hazardous environments such

as factories. If your business will have five or more employees then you will need to record the results of your **risk assessment**. Following the risk assessment, employers need to:

- put in place H&S measures identified as necessary by the risk assessment

- appoint competent people to implement these H&S measures

- implement emergency procedures

- provide training (and clear information) to employees

- work with any other employers that share the same workplace

Bear in mind that H&S measures need to be matched to the levels of risk involved. For example, accident records reflect that the manufacturing sector had 10 times more accidents than the office sector. But don't panic, they are still both relatively safe places to work; there were under 600 accidents requiring more than 3 days off work per 100,000 people employed in Great Britain according to the latest statistics.

First-Aid at work is covered by The Health and Safety (First-Aid) Regulations 1981. This requires an employer to provide "*adequate and appropriate equipment, facilities and personnel to enable first aid to be given to your employees if they are injured or become ill at work.*" Of course, what is adequate and appropriate will be related to the type of work that your business does and should have been addressed in the risk assessment. As a bare minimum, the employer must provide:

- a first-aid box that is suitably stocked; you may need more than one of these to be located at appropriate places throughout your premises

- an appointed person to handle what happens if someone is hurt or falls ill at work; this may mean more than one person to cover holidays etc. The same person should have responsibility for re-stocking the first-aid box after use; don't forget that certain items in the first-aid box may have a shelf-life and will need replacing every so often.

Don't forget that injury and illness can happen at any time so it's no use keeping a first-aid box in an office that is locked when people are still at work. A **First-Aider** (again you may need more than one) is someone trained with first-aid knowledge and who holds a current first aid at work certificate awarded following attendance at a HSE approved course.

FIRST AID AT WORK

You may have seen one of the 'Emergency First-Aid' posters at work. This is important stuff. One of our professional advisers here at Business Boffins saved the life of a lady who collapsed in the street. He was able to do so because he had read the poster at work.

Three cheers for him!

Why not put an additional poster just by where the kettle boils at work? Putting it up may be the best 10 minutes you ever spend.

We must say that we think the HSE is *fab*; their website is really excellent with loads of downloadable leaflets and guidance and you really must ask your local HSE office (see "Yellow Pages") for any advice that you may require. We think the HSE is doing a great job – three cheers for them! Specific things to draw your attention to are:

- download the leaflet **homeworking.pdf** from the HSE website if you are **working from home**; it tells you exactly what you need to know and has some useful information about visual display units (VDUs) which is another term for your computer screen.

- similarly, download the leaflet **officewise.pdf** from the HSE website if you propose to run an office. Once again, it contains excellent guidance for employers and employees.

- we also recommend that you download the leaflet **PPE.pdf** from the HSE website which is a short guide to **Personal Protective Equipment (PPE)** such as safety glasses and hard hats *etc.*

This latter leaflet neatly links us to the next section about using equipment at work.

EQUIPMENT AT WORK

Almost anything used at work may be considered to be work equipment. Even a pencil can cause injury at work if you stick it in someone's arm. Although, to be honest, I haven't seen that happen since the third form at school.

You will need to look at all the equipment that will be used in your business as part of your risk assessment. It's convenient to develop a spreadsheet, or ideally a database, to do this. The following is a simple example as a guide:

1. Equipment: **2. Uses:**

1 Circular saw   Ripping wood

etc...

When you've pulled that together, add two more columns as follows:

3. Risks: **4. Preventive Action:**

Fence loose   Inspect fence /adjust

Bearings worn   Grease bearings monthly

Waste underfoot   (i) Install dust extractor

          (ii) Sweep area regularly

Using this approach, you can develop a simple database that evolves as you add more equipment. You will need to use this as a management tool which is to say that you must review if **everything** is being done to sensibly avoid risk and, if not, then do what else is required.

In addition to this risk assessment, you must also look to see if the **right equipment is being used for the right task.** And you must also ensure that:

- equipment is properly maintained and calibrated

- all necessary safety devices are installed and working

- all employees are properly trained in the use of, for example, a machine before they operate it

You must also ensure that the right information and instructions are provided with all equipment so that the user can check anything they are unsure of. Remember that no matter how good you feel your training provision is, people can forget things. That doesn't mean they are poor employees – it means they are human! A poor employee would be someone who doesn't ask when they are unsure. And that makes them an unsafe employee too.

Don't forget about the type of work that will have to be done when maintaining equipment. Things can get awfully dangerous when taken to pieces. Especially electrical items. And don't forget that allowing waste or debris to accumulate makes operating equipment dangerous too. So ensure that procedures are in place to remove waste. Now these are only general guidelines about Health and Safety, more information can be found on the HSE website. But don't forget that your local H&S office can help with any questions that you may have. Remember, "it's better to be safe than sorry".

FINANCING

If you've read the chapter 'Basic Accounting' you will know that things like buildings and big pieces of equipment are categorised by accountants as Capital Items which means that they come under Fixed Assets. Now these types of things usually cost lots of money to buy. And so it's worth just taking a moment in this chapter to think about how you intend to finance the purchase of a big **Capital Expense** like a building or a delivery van. Few businesses these days go and buy an office building when they start off. And the reason is **cash flow**.

If your business starts off with £200,000 in the business account, is it really sensible to go and blow all of that cash on an office building? Probably not. Would it be better to rent a building and use the cash for operating expenses until you have the business up and running? Probably yes. Could you achieve the same thing by buying the office premises using a mortgage? Well yes, you could, but your business may not be able to get a mortgage if you are starting off and have no evidence of trading, ie the mortgage company would find it hard to confirm that your new business would be capable of paying the mortgage repayments since there would be no evidence of income to date.

And so there exist a variety of finance mechanisms available now to assist you and your business make best use of business capital – sometimes it's best to use business capital to buy an item, sometimes it's best to rent, lease or hire purchase an item. Inevitably, your accountant will advise you about what to do regarding finances. But what finance 'products' are available? Here's an overview of the two main options that your accountant may advise you to consider:

- **Hire Purchase** (HP) involves the purchase of an item over a period of time. The 'hirer' pays an initial deposit and the remaining balance (plus interest) in staged payments over a period of time. Although more expensive (because of interest), hire purchase offers several advantages for a small business:

  1. the item can be used immediately

  2. payments are made over a period of time so cash flow is improved

  3. the hirer can recover 'depreciation' costs and VAT

  However, one thing to bear in mind is that the finance company (the 'creditor') owns the item until the last payment has been made.

- **Leasing** is different in that it is a contract between you, the 'lessee', and the finance house, the 'lessor'. A **finance lease** is when the value of the rental over the rental period is equal to, or greater than, 90% of the cost of the item. An **operating lease** is more like a **rental** in that the item has a resale value at the end of the lease; commonly this is **contract hire** for such things as company cars. However, this concept is the same as renting a building; you pay to use the building and then vacate it (hand it back) at the end of the rental period.

IN SUMMARY

This chapter has:

- looked at the different forms of business premises that are available

- summarised aspects of Health and Safety appropriate for buildings and equipment

- reviewed finance options for capital items

Many of these topics are important considerations when you plan your new business and all should be addressed when you write your business plan.

In business, things can and do go wrong. Things that you can't plan for. Things that you wouldn't in your wildest dreams imagine would happen. But they do. Fortunately, such things don't happen very often. And as they don't, insurers are able to use historic records to take a judgement on the likelihood of a potential risk happening in certain circumstances (you can't insure against the vague notion of a 'problem', it has to be a defined incident arising in specific circumstances).

The good news is that the less the likelihood, then the less the risk and of course the lower the cost of insurance as a proportion of what it would cost to correct the problem. Which is why, of course, it usually costs more for people who jump out of aircraft to obtain life insurance than for people who don't. Although it is often argued that parachuting is a comparatively safe sport (since accidents don't often arise) the consequences of a parachute not opening are usually rather severe. On the other hand, an ankle injury from a bad landing after a parachute jump may be more frequent but less severe.

So could one insure against death that resulted from a parachute not opening? And could one insure against an ankle injury from a bad landing? Whilst the answer is probably yes to both questions it's useful to consider what the insurer will think about in setting the charge for insurance. First off, how often do these things happen? Secondly, have you taken steps to use the right equipment from a reputable supplier? Thirdly, have you got the appropriate training for the task?

So from this perhaps unusual example, it is clear that insurers must consider a range of factors:

- frequency of parachutes failing

- frequency of the person's exposure to the event (how many time a year they jump)

- quality of materials used in the parachute

- training and experience of the person

And not surprisingly, the approach to business insurance is very similar; a variety of factors are considered when insuring against a specific business risk. In this chapter we will look at some of the common forms of business insurance.

WHAT IS RISK?

An old martial arts instructor once said that, "the best way to avoid a punch is to not be there." So, apart from having the slightly annoying habit of talking like Yoda in Star Wars, the wisdom of the old man was the advice that minimising exposure to risk is a lot better than having to deal with the consequences. Sounds obvious. Well it is, but only if you are aware of the risk in the first place. And learning about the different forms of risk in business is a central theme of the Business Boffins programme — 'avoid the avoidable.'

Business planning involves trying to assess, and then minimise, risk in the business — this usually means reducing the risk of losing money

Much of the inherent risk with a business should be addressed in the business plan (some business gurus use the ugly term 'de-risking' the business). Planning how you will handle a variety of known challenges is all part of the business planning process. Like doing market research to avoid the risk that nobody wants to buy your product, no matter how wonderful you may think it is. And doing competitor research to check that nobody is about to launch a product just like yours. But cheaper.

As we have said, some things happen that you simply can't plan for. And that is where insurance comes in. Many types of business risk can be insured against but the insurer may require, or even insist, that your business take steps to reduce the risk. In addition, you may be able to get lower insurance premiums if the business takes steps to improve security or to increase safety through staff training for example. But whilst it's up to you to choose which of the many types of business insurance will be sensible for your business, some types of business insurance are a legal requirement.

So let's start with them.

STATUTORY INSURANCE

It is a legal requirement for all employers to insure against their legal responsibility for death, accident or disease sustained by employees as a consequence of their employment. You must display this certificate of insurance at the workplace for all to see. The level of insurance cover is usually around £10 million pounds. This is termed **'Employer's Liability Insurance'**. Since this is obviously very important, let's look at it in a little more detail.

EMPLOYER'S LIABILITY

With few exceptions ALL EMPLOYERS must have employer's liability insurance BY LAW. This insurance provides protection against legal liability for injury to employees and the current MINIMUM level of cover required is £5,000,000 per any one occurrence. Insurers usually give an automatic amount of £10,000,000 per occurrence, with the option to increase this if required. Standard protection includes:

- Legal costs for actions brought under 'The Health and Safety at Work Act'

- 'Indemnity to principal' if required by a contract for work away from premises

- Worldwide cover for employees normally resident in the UK

- Unsatisfied court judgements

MOTOR VEHICLES

The Road Traffic Act makes it clear that third party motor insurance must be in place before a vehicle is used on the road. This applies even if a vehicle is unlicensed or does not need to be registered for tax purposes. In law, a road is described as any highway or other road to which the public has access. Even Contractors Plant such as forklift trucks used on partially completed housing estates and unfinished or unadopted roads **must have this cover.** Agricultural vehicles often do not need road fund licenses if they are used on public roads simply to pass from one part of a farmer's land to another, but they **still require compulsory motor insurance.**

STATUTORY INSPECTION OF PLANT & MACHINERY

Certain types of Plant and Machinery have to be inspected BY LAW to meet safety criteria. These inspections must be carried out by a competent person. Amongst the items are:

- Boilers & pressure vessels including compressors/air receivers, steam pressure plant & sterilisation equipment such as Autoclaves

- Certain electrical, welding and mechanical plant

- Cranes, lifts and lifting plant, such as forklifts and electrical/manual lifting gear and tackle

- Fume/vapour extraction

- Air conditioning /refrigeration plant

There are several providers of this service, and sometimes the company that supplies and maintains the equipment can also provide the inspection service.

OTHER FORMS OF INSURANCE

There are many other forms of business insurance that can be obtained as a way of protecting against potential risk. Some of these seem more or less essential for most businesses whilst others will clearly be optional. A list of potentially important insurance types to consider would include the following:

- **Property damage & theft** (buildings & contents, and portable items used away from your premises)

- **Business interruption** (loss of revenue/gross profit or increased costs of working). You should also consider having a *Disaster Recovery and Business Continuity Plan*.

- **Public liability**

- **Products liability** (where relevant to your business)

- **Professional indemnity** (malpractice)

- **Intellectual property/patents**

Other forms of more optional insurance would include the following:

- **Book debts/outstanding debit balances**

- **Money** (at your premises and in transit)

- **Deterioration of stock** (damage and loss of revenue arising from)

- **Machinery breakdown** (rectification costs & loss of revenue)

- **Computer breakdown** (rectification costs & loss of revenue)

- **Loss of statutory licence**

- **Legal expenses**

- **Goods in transit** (UK & abroad, including imports/exports)

- **Credit insurance** (bad debts/debt recovery)

- **Travel insurance** (group & individual, and available on an annual basis or one-off trips)

- **Directors' & officers' liability**

- **Personal accident and optional sickness benefit**

- **Private medical** (BUPA *etc*)

- **Product recall and/or product guarantee**

RISK MANAGEMENT

The process of systematically reviewing the critical aspects of your business, and what risks are involved, is a sensible one to undertake at the outset. Putting appropriate insurance in place is one aspect of risk management. Another aspect is to use the process to identify weaknesses that can be corrected in a way that reduces risk; for example, staff training or tighter security measures.

You should note that any business with five or more employees, including the Principal(s) or Director(s), is required by law to have in place a written Health & Safety (H&S) Policy, which must be available for inspection, if required, by the relevant Authority. Guidance can be obtained from the Health & Safety Executive, but there are specialist Personnel, Employment Law and Health & Safety Consultancies who, for a fee, will help set up the H&S procedures and also advise on Employment Law and will assist in writing Employment Contracts too.

Whilst on this note of health, it's important to think about health insurance as a form of risk management. What would happen to your business if members of staff were to have a long-term illness for example? Or, God forbid, even to die? Let's start with the worst case of death - this is covered by a 'Death in Service' scheme. And don't forget that it is helpful to look at this both from the employer's and employee's perspective.

DEATH IN SERVICE SCHEME

Employer's Considerations:

- A Death in Service scheme provides a valuable benefit that can help attract and retain high quality staff.

- Corporation tax relief is normally available on premiums paid on behalf of employees

- The provision of cover resolves the emotive moral and financial question of how to provide support to the deceased's family.

- Administration is kept to a minimum and the claims procedure is fast and straightforward.

Employee's Perspectives

- Death in Service benefits, paid through a cash lump sum and/or dependants' pension, ensure that an employee's dependants are looked after in the event of the employee's death.

- Premiums paid into the scheme on behalf of the employee will not be taxed as a benefit in kind.

- Benefits are normally paid immediately via the trustees and are usually free of inheritance tax.

- In the majority of cases, employees will not have to complete a medical questionnaire.

- An employee who has been unable to take out individual cover may be eligible for cover under a group scheme.

A Death in Service Scheme can be established on the basis of a lump sum benefit of either 1, 2, 3 or 4 times salary. But this form of scheme is not the only one available to cover health issues. Another form of scheme that pays money to the business is 'Key-person' insurance.

KEY-PERSON INSURANCE

More and more businesses are realising the importance of their employees and as such are taking out insurance on them in the form of Key-Person cover. Whereas a company has normally only considered insuring their stock, machinery and vehicles, it is becoming apparent to many that their most important asset is their workforce, or at least the more senior categories of that workforce.

Problems caused by the loss of a Key-Person due to death or illness may be categorised into four major areas:

- **Loss of profits**

- **Loan security**

- **Investment protection**

- **Management buy-outs**

Historically, companies have only concerned themselves with death, but once again attitudes are changing in that more are now also considering the implications of a critical illness. Just take a look at some of the statistics and judge for yourself...

- More than 1 in 2 people in the UK will be affected by diseases such as cancer & heart disease

- 1 in 8 males aged 30 will contract cancer before the age of 65

- 1 in 5 males aged 30 will suffer a heart attack before the age of 65

For example, you could have a heart attack and be unable to return to work either in the short to medium term, or indeed at all, but with a pure life assurance risk contract no benefit would be payable.

Obviously the cost increases quite substantially by including critical illness, as the risk is far higher as statistically it is more likely to occur. The type of cover chosen to be most appropriate can vary from person to person (as with the sum assured); depending on how "key" they are to the business. Should you feel critical illness is important, but where you would also like to restrict the cost, another option would be to have a reduced sum assured benefit payable in respect of critical illness, eg say £250,000 payable in the event of death, but say, only £100,000 in respect of critical illness.

Having considered the impact of the death of a key employee, or even the diagnosis of a critical illness, it is also important to look at the impact of a key employee being unable to work because of sickness or an accident.

EXECUTIVE PERMANENT HEALTH INSURANCE (PHI)

Most businesses would want to be able to keep paying a valued employee until he or she was well enough to return to work but not all would be able to afford it. If the employee's sickness was prolonged, there would come a time when the dilemma of when to stop paying them would have to be faced. For senior employees, a long period of illness without adequate financial protection could put them in real financial hardship. State benefits for ill health are principally designed to avoid poverty and do not provide sufficient income to maintain most people's standard of living.

An employee's prolonged absence from work will result in new 'hidden' costs, such as hiring a replacement, training new staff, lower productivity of replacement staff, overtime payments, and supervisory time. Maintaining an employee's salary on top of these costs puts extra pressure on the company's resources at a time when the employee is unable to contribute to the profitability of the business.

Executive Permanent Health Insurance (PHI) can be taken out by a company on the life of most full time employees below the age of 55, although employers usually restrict cover to their working directors or senior executives. A business can usually have up to four plans at any one time, as once considerations are given to providing protection for more than four employees, a group scheme could be established.

Executive PHI provides the financial means to help maintain your employees' salaries while they're ill — and in the most tax efficient way:

- Safeguarding the company's financial resources

- Maintaining your employees' lifestyles during illness

- Increasing company loyalty and commitment amongst employees.

Benefits would become payable (after the selected deferred period) in the event that the employee is totally unable to do his or her own specific job, and is of course, not doing another. This benefit would continue to be made until (i) the employee recovers and returns to work, (ii) the plan expires (cover is usually provided until the company's normal retirement age) or, (iii) the employee dies. Should the employee return to work, but due to the illness or disability, is unable to return to his or her own specific job, and returns in a part-time capacity or has to take a less well paid position, a reduced benefit would be payable.

DIRECTOR/PARTNERSHIP PROTECTION

With the best will in the world, things can go wrong. People change. Their aspirations and priorities change, their circumstances change and previously close, working relationships can sometimes sour. Whilst this is unfortunate enough in personal friendships, when it happens in business relationships it can be terminal.

For this reason, it is necessary to have in place a clear, legally binding understanding between directors or partners in a business that stipulates what will happen if one of them dies or wishes to sell up, or falls into dispute with the other(s). With careful planning and the right types of insurance, it is possible to protect yourself and your business against the implications of most common scenarios, including death in service and legal expenses.

The extent to which your business may be exposed in the event of a director or partner dying or wishing to sell their shares depends on the care with which your original agreement was drawn up. As always, we advise that you consult your lawyer and your accountant and, armed with their advice, then speak with an independent financial adviser

DIRECTORS' AND OFFICERS' LIABILITY INSURANCE

This category of insurance relates to those involved with the running of a limited company. Every person holding the office of Director or Officer of a company assumes substantial personal liability. This form of insurance is taken out to protect Directors and Officers against this liability. The insurance cover might be up to £20 million, for example, for any one risk.

So far we have looked at statutory insurance requirements and those relating primarily to people. Most people will be familiar with insurance relating to things (like houses, cars and freezers) and, not surprisingly, there are many forms of business insurance that fall into this category. Here are some of the common ones:

MONEY-RELATED INSURANCE

It is possible to insure against **cash loss,** either held at your business premises or in transit, being lost or stolen. Less obvious is insurance against people not paying your bills. **Book debts** or **credit insurance** fall into this category.

BUSINESS INTERRUPTION INSURANCE

It is possible to take out a comprehensive business interruption policy that will insure against a wide variety of different forms of things that might disrupt, or even halt, your business activities. It is also possible to insure against specific things that might disrupt your business; **computer breakdown** or other **machinery breakdown** for example.

PROBLEMS WITH STOCK

Apart from the obvious perils of Fire, Theft and Water Damage etc other unforeseen circumstances can lead to a **deterioration of stock;** for example, stock could be ruined following damage to, or breakdown of, temperature controlled units. Such an event can have a very dramatic effect on certain types of business and, once again, this can be insured against. Anything from ice cream to drugs and experimental research material.

PREMISES

An obvious form of insurance is that related to your business **premises.** These insurance formats can cover issues relating to break-ins and malicious damage through to destruction caused by severe weather.

COMBINED PACKAGES

Many insurers now offer combined packages of insurance structured for a particular type of business; examples include hotels and restaurants, surgeries, retail outlets and public houses.

CONCLUSION

Risk assessment is an important part of the business planning process. An independent financial adviser can therefore contribute to your business plan by helping you to assess risk and insurance needs.

HOMEWORK TIME...

Make a list of all the major activities that you expect to undertake when you run your business. Try to consider all risks associated with those major activities. Can you take steps to reduce risk for any activity? This is a process that you may need to go through several times as you (i) think of new activities and (ii) think of new ways to avoid, or minimise, associated risks.

When you've got as far as you can with this process, try to prioritise the risks in terms of impact upon your business. It may be useful to prioritise them in terms of 'critical', 'major' and 'minor' business impact. With that prioritised list you now have a tool with which to discuss your insurance needs with an Independent Financial Adviser. Don't be afraid to ask their advice about things that you may have forgotten. Watch out though, in our experience many of them can "talk for England". Getting quotes for the various insurance protections that you may need will allow you to feed those costs into your cash flow forecast when we get to chapter 11.

There is nothing magical or complicated about setting a budget. All that is required is a logical and realistic approach to financing. The most important form of budget, in our view, is the cash flow forecast. In approaching this budget, it is important to have considered all of the likely expenditure and when that is likely to fall due for payment. All estimates of income must be realistic as well. By putting this all together you can estimate what money is required, and when, for your business.

WHAT IS A CASH FLOW FORECAST?

Quite simply a cash flow forecast is used to estimate what money will come into, or go out of, the business bank account on a month-by-month basis. And so if, in one month, an overdraft requirement is predicted then this can be discussed with the bank manager ahead of that need. The cash flow forecast looks at *what will happen*, rather than *what has happened* and so takes no account of what the business has done historically. It's therefore not a measure of the value or of the assets of the company but more of its predicted performance. Let's look at a simple example:

Cash flow forecast for Whizzo Wedding Planners Ltd - first half of 2007

	Jan (£)	Feb (£)	Mar (£)	Apr (£)	May (£)	Jun (£)	HALF-YEAR TOTALS (£)
Income:							
Investment capital	10,000	0	0	0	0	0	10,000
Sales	0	0	0	2,500	4,500	5,750	12,750
TOTAL IN:	**10,000**	**0**	**0**	**2,500**	**4,500**	**5,750**	**22,750**
Outgoings:							
Professional fees	750	225	0	0	0	0	975
Computer hardware	3,750	0	0	0	0	0	3,750
Office rental	350	350	350	350	350	350	2,100
Phone	150	150	150	175	175	175	975
Internet charges	15	15	15	15	15	15	90
Design costs	1,250	0	0	0	0	0	1,250
Printing costs	0	3,575	0	0	0	0	3,575
Stationery	120	120	80	80	80	80	560
Travel costs	125	125	125	225	225	225	1,050
Wages	1,500	1,500	1,500	1,500	1,500	1,500	9,000
National Insurance	195	195	195	195	195	195	1,170
Expenses	125	125	125	125	125	125	750
TOTAL OUT	**8,330**	**6,380**	**2,540**	**2,665**	**2,665**	**2,665**	**25,245**
MONTHLY CASH FLOW:	**1,670**	-6,380	-2,540	-165	**1,835**	**3,085**	
MONTHLY BANK BALANCE:	**1,670**	-4,710	-7,250	-7,415	-5,580	-2,495	

Having scared you with a table of numbers on the first page of this chapter please don't panic. This example is only a very simple one that covers the first six months of a new business. The business employs two people, each drawing a modest income of £9,000 per year. The two directors of the company each invested £5,000 into the business at the outset giving the investment capital of £10,000.

They rented a small office in a local 'incubator facility' that offered several support services apart from just office space such as access to a meetings room and a receptionist at the front door. The offices already had office furniture which was also a help. And the rent also included business rates. They felt that this sort of facility, coupled with them starting a limited company, gave the right kind of impression to clients. Having spent some time with an accountant and a solicitor they kicked off the business.

In the first month of operations they bought and installed a computer and commissioned a design company to come up with designs for their brochures. The two directors felt that a good brochure was important in order to attract the kind of client that they expected. The cash flow forecast predicted all of this for the first month but also forecast what expenditure and income was likely in the first six months. The pair were realistic and did not include any 'sales' for three months; they figured it would take them that long to get going and that weddings had a 'seasonal component' in any case with most taking place in the summer months.

Armed with their business plan and the cash flow forecast the two realised that they would not be able to survive on the £10,000 initial investment and went to see their bank manager. The bank manager was pleased to see that the pair had put some of their own money into the business and that it was well thought out. Their accountant had advised them that they had two opportunities at the bank to make up the negative position that their finances hit in February onwards (i) a business loan to be paid back over, say, three years or (ii) an overdraft facility. Having reviewed the options and armed with market research data, the directors felt that they did not need a business loan but that a short-term overdraft would be adequate.

The reason for this was that they expected their business to become profitable by May and that they would be "back in the black" during the second half of the year. However, their bank manager had other ideas: he offered a business loan of £8,000 that would cover even their worst month (April) when they predicted that the business would be £7,355 'in the red'. He also offered them a rather expensive business loan repayment protection policy to insure against not being able to meet the repayments. But he didn't offer them the overdraft. Unperturbed, the pair went to a second high street bank manager recommended by their accountant. They also smartened up their market research data before the meeting and specifically asked for an overdraft, explaining why they felt confident that a business loan was unnecessary. This time the bank manager was in agreement and opened up a business bank account with an agreed overdraft of £8,000 with that facility to be reviewed again in six month's time. They did have to give personal guarantees for the overdraft facility but that did not give either of them cause for concern, since, if the worst thing happened, they both had cars that could be sold to cover the £8,000, ie neither would lose their home!

PREPARING THE CASH FLOW FORECAST

Now this form of cash flow forecast is one of the simplest that you could use. It would cope with the majority of small businesses with a few modifications. But small businesses that sell a service usually have quite a simple cash flow forecast. For example, 'Whizzo Wedding Planners' had no raw materials since they didn't manufacture a product but rather sold a service. Hence there were no manufacturing costs in their cash flow forecast. Things start to get a bit more complicated for manufacturing businesses, but not overly so. The best place to start with the cash flow forecast is with expenditure. Start by costing out all of the things that you will need to pay for in order to run your business. We see three categories of expenditure:

1. **Capital expenditure** — those things like big machines, vehicles, computers or office furniture that you will need (usually immediately) in order to operate as a business

2. **Operating expenditure** — the costs incurred as you go along including raw materials, wages, telephone charges, rental costs *etc*

3. **External contracts** — those payments that are made to people to whom you sub-contract specific work out to; but work related to your product (*ie* not your brochure printer)

When you've completed that process, look next at income from sales. When will your business begin to make sales of your product or service? Probably not in the first month. And you may not really get going for three or even six months due to production lead-in times (how long it takes to manufacture, package and distribute products for example) or due to the impact of an advertising campaign.

Having fed your sales figures into the cash flow forecast you will then be able to see what shortfalls there are in the cash flow of the business for the first year (*although the 'Whizzo Wedding Planners' example was for a six-month period we always suggest that you plan for a year at a time*). Typically this means how much money will be required 'up-front' in order to start off the business.

Most businesses require some 'set-up' capital to get going — even if that is only to pay for office furniture and a computer for example. From your cash flow forecast you'll know how much is required and can then take a view as to how to raise that cash. Will that cash come from your own savings, from an investor or from a bank loan? Or will an overdraft facility be appropriate? These decisions are much easier to make by using a cash flow forecast. And of course, your accountant will advise you on this. The accountant may also point out ways in which you can organise or schedule your cash flow to be more helpful for the business (for example, you may not need to buy all of the machines that you require in one month, especially if each one takes some weeks to install). And the accountant will probably spot one or two things that you have forgotten to include.

Let's now take a look at a slightly more complicated cash flow forecast on the next page — *you will need to refer back to this page as you work through the remainder of this chapter.*

	Jan	Feb	Mar	Apr	May	Jun	Jul	Aug	Sep	Oct	Nov	Dec	TOTALS
Investment capital	150,000												150,000
Sales-product 1 (add rows as req'd)		4,000	8,600	9,750	11,000	12,000	12,000	15,000	19,500	26,400	28,750	26,470	173,470
Sales-service 1 (add rows as req'd)				550	650	750	1,000	1,100	1,250	1,600	1,950	1,600	10,450
TOTAL CASH FLOW IN	150,000	4,000	8,600	10,300	11,650	12,750	13,000	16,100	20,750	28,000	30,700	28,070	333,920
Capital expenditure (CapEx)													
Premises													0
Vehicles		12,000											12,000
Office equipment	5,500	3,500	500	750					350			620	11,220
Manufacturing Equipment	37,500	3,575	750	1,275	325	1,855							45,280
CapEx TOTAL	43,000	19,075	1,250	2,025	325	1,855	0	0	350	0	0	620	68,500
Operating expenditure (OpEx)													
Salaries (gross amount totals)	9,500	11,000	11,000	13,000	13,000	13,000	13,000	14,500	14,500	14,500	14,500	14,500	156,000
National insurance (13%)	1,235	1,430	1,430	1,690	1,690	1,690	1,690	1,885	1,885	1,885	1,885	1,885	20,280
Pensions (5%)	475	550	550	650	650	650	650	725	725	725	725	725	7,800
Life cover scheme	250	275	275	325	325	325	325	350	350	350	350	350	3,850
Rent	1,800	1,800	1,800	1,800	1,800	1,800	1,800	1,800	1,800	1,800	1,800	1,800	21,600
Rates	250	250	250	250	250	250	250	250	250	250	250	250	3,000
Combined business insurance	350	350	350	350	350	350	350	350	350	350	350	350	4,200
Utilities	180	180	180	180	180	180	180	180	180	180	180	180	2,160
Phone	120	120	120	120	120	120	120	120	120	120	120	120	1,440
Legal & intellectual property	3,000				2,000					3,000			8,000
Accounting, payroll & audit charges	1,200	50	50	50	50	50	50	50	50	50	2,550	50	4,250
Business travel	100	100	100	100	100	500	500	100	100	100	100	100	2,000
Bank charges	25	25	25	25	25	25	25	25	25	25	25	25	300
Health and safety	500	500	250	100	100	100	100	100	100	100	100	100	2,150
Stationery	100	100	100	100	100	100	100	100	100	100	100	100	1,200
Raw materials	5,870	4,380	1,250	1,250	1,250	1,250	1,250	1,250	1,250	1,250	1,250	1,250	22,750
OpEx TOTAL	24,955	21,110	17,730	19,990	21,990	20,390	20,390	21,785	21,785	24,785	24,285	21,785	260,980
TOTAL CASH FLOW OUT	67,955	40,185	18,980	22,015	22,315	22,245	20,390	21,785	22,135	24,785	24,285	22,405	329,480
MONTHLY NET CASH FLOW	82,045	-36,185	-10,380	-11,715	-10,665	-9,495	-7,390	-5,685	-1,385	3,215	6,415	5,665	
MONTHLY BANK BALANCE	82,045	45,860	35,480	23,765	13,100	3,605	-3,785	-9,470	-10,855	-7,640	-1,225	4,440	

This fairly generic cash flow forecast template should be suitable, with modification, for the majority of small businesses and we would suggest that you create one in Excel. The overall format is really no different from that on the first page of this chapter; it lists categories of cash in and cash out down the left hand column and then allows numbers to be entered (against each month) across the columns. And the best thing about a spreadsheet is that it adds up for you ("Hurrah" for Excel).

The example business has ten employees and is a manufacturing business. An initial investment of £150,000 has been arranged in order to kick the business off. Let's take a look at the cash flow forecast in detail — starting at the top, and work our way down as follows:

The first row relates to investment capital; that is money invested in the business. *This may have come from money put into the business by the owners or it might have come from private investors including friends and family. Alternatively, any cash coming into the business as a loan, instead of an investment, could go here or in a new row inserted before sales.*

The template lists rows for just one product and one service — please duplicate these as required. Some people just have a single row for 'sales', others like to be able to predict sales for a particular product or service. The choice is yours, but forecasting for *each* product or service allows you to look at performance more easily as the business gets going. Of course, this becomes impractical if you have hundreds of products; better then to group them into meaningful categories.

Hence the total of cash flow in to the business is shown in the next row. What is clear from this row is that the business is forecasting that sales will increase as the year goes on (with a slight dip for December which reflects the Christmas period). This sort of forecast is very sensible since it shows that sales take some time to build up. Overall, this business is predicting that £333,920 will flow into the business, of which £150,000 is investment capital and the rest is cash received from sales.

Turning to the next row we see that this relates to items of capital expenditure. There is nothing in the row for premises because (i) the premises are rented and (ii) nothing had to be spent on converting them when the business moved in. The main purchases are office equipment and manufacturing equipment. The business took the decision to buy a second hand delivery van for £12,000 rather than leasing a new van.

Please also note that the business bought the equipment outright as well — this is one option but many businesses nowadays elect to lease major equipment or to arrange hire purchase in order to spread costs over a period of time. By spreading payments over, for example, a three year period this business would have required less investment capital at the outset. Nevertheless, for some businesses outright purchase is appropriate; particularly when machinery is being bought second-hand.

The next section covers operating expenditure, those costs associated with running the business. The first item in this section is salaries; this is the total of all salaries before the deduction of any tax or national insurance that the employee must pay (termed gross salary). Below this row is the amount of national insurance that an employer must pay every month, which is approximately 13% of gross salaries at the current time.

The next two rows relate to a pension scheme that the business has set up as well as a life cover scheme. The business contributes 5% of gross salary for each employee towards the pension scheme. Typically the employee would contribute 5% of salary as well; those costs do not appear on the cash flow forecast since they come out of gross salary which is already included. *Incidentally, that is also why there is no allocation for income tax — that comes out of gross salary as well.* The life cover scheme is paid for by the business and provides a lump sum for dependants of the employee in the event of death in service.

The amount allocated to rent is self-explanatory although it should be noted that rent often includes more than simple floor-space these days; typically, the rent may include cleaning services, waste disposal and, for large facilities, access to things like meeting rooms and a tea-room or even a canteen. Some rents also include a component for business rates but this business lists those as separate charges.

A combined **business insurance** package has been opted for by this business; this will include statutory insurance as well as a range of other insurances appropriate for this type of business.

Utilities relate to gas, water, electricity etc and may be a combined service charge from the landlord of the rented premises; this is especially true when facilities are shared by several small businesses. It's normal for each business in rented facilities to pay for their own **telephone** use however since this varies dramatically between businesses.

This business has incorporated **legal costs** and **intellectual property costs** together — this is because they use the same firm of lawyers for both. The amounts allocated for **accounting** also includes a sum for the monthly production of '**payroll**', the calculation of salaries and deductions and the preparation of 'wage slips', together with an allowance for **auditing**.

Business travel is always a difficult thing to budget for and often contentious with employees. We think that all employees should have the same travel perks — having bosses fly "Club Class" and other employees fly "Economy Class" is always damaging to staff morale. An estimate of £100 per month won't go far these days although it's noted that £500 / month has been allocated for June and July; typically this might relate to attendance at a trade conference for example.

Bank charges here are nominal — costs of cheques etc but note that most banks now offer free business banking for at least the first year. Take note also that no recognition of bank interest (paid or payable) has been included in this cash flow forecast.

Health and safety costs relate to a variety of things including the undertaking of risk assessments and the costs of staff training for example.

Stationery covers pretty much all 'consumables' in an office ranging from printed letter heads to pencils. Many direct mail order suppliers now also supply coffee as well.

Raw materials cover all of those things that are bought and then used to make your product. For this business, what is clear is that the cost of raw materials (£1,250 per month) is only around 1/20th of the sales income by the end of the year. This clearly indicates that the business adds a great deal of 'value' to the product during the production process.

Finally, are there any omissions from the spreadsheet that look obvious? Well yes; here are a few other items that could be included:

- design costs

- printed material (letterheads & brochures)

- website construction and hosting

- internet service provision

- advertising

- staff training

- staff welfare (covers matters arising on a compassionate basis)

- VAT (if your sales projections include VAT then you will need to include a row in your operating expenditure for your VAT payments to HM Revenue & Customs)

However, the spreadsheet takes no account of 'surprises' or costs that arise that cannot be predicted. It's hard to give hard and fast rules about what to allocate as a contingency but we think that 5% of the overall budget is about right. More than 10% as a contingency means that you have not gone through the budget exercise with enough care! So we would have expected a contingency of around £16,000 in the budget being 5% of overall costs.

WHAT DOES THE CASH FLOW FORECAST TELL ME?

Actually, quite a lot. Let's look at some of the summary totals. To start with, we can see that the total cash flow in is £333,920 which is just greater than the total cash flow out of £329,480. The difference is £4,440 which ties in exactly with what is in the business account at the end of December. But what is apparent also is that of the cash flow in, some £150,000 came from investment capital. In other words, the business has spent more than it earned. Is this a problem?

Well, we can address that question by looking at the cash flow in and out during the later months; we see that there is a trend in October, November and December for the business to generate *more* cash flow in than cash flow out. Phew! That's a good thing since it means that the business has become profitable by the fourth quarter of the year. But note that this doesn't mean that the business has cash in the bank. In fact, the business is overdrawn in October. But at least the cash flow forecast allows discussion with the bank, at an early stage, about an overdraft facility for the months of July through to October. And that advanced notice is very helpful at the bank — bank managers don't like surprises.

Clearly, taking £160,000 as investment capital would have avoided the need for an overdraft altogether. However, it's quite frequent for this sort of situation to arise, usually for one of three reasons:

- the investment capital represents the maximum that the owners could raise (in this case £150,000)

- the owners take less investment capital at the start and rely more heavily on a bank loan or an extended overdraft at the bank (which costs more in interest and bank charges)

- the owners of a limited company only issue shares to a set limit which represents how much of the company they are prepared to release into other people's ownership (quite often less than 50%) which can limit the cash raised

CONCLUSIONS

We think that the cash flow forecast is a vital, and incredibly useful, piece of work that must be done before you start your business. It will allow you to budget and control your finances and it's a performance measurement tool with which to assess how your business is performing.

If time doesn't permit everything, make sure that the cash flow forecast for your business isn't skipped!

John Harcourt decided to set up a computer consultancy, which he would run essentially on his own. Although, after due thought, John decided that he ought to have an administrator join him perhaps six months after he started. John started off by looking at his personal outgoings and decided that his business would need to pay him £25,000 per year in order to cover his family costs. So he decided to make it £26,000 to give a bit extra to be on the safe side. He figured that an administrator could work from 09:30 until 15:30, which he hoped, would fit with a working parent who needed to drop off and pick up children from school. So he reckoned around £12,000 per year would be reasonable for those hours. He plugged those costs into the **headcount/payroll** spreadsheet and had himself starting in month one and the administrator in month seven.

Next, John started to build the main **cash flow forecast** and began with his **Operating Expenditure (OpEx).** He added the total salary bill as a single line but did not include tax or employee's national insurance since that would be deducted from the gross pay and could therefore be ignored. But he did remember to add a line for employer's national insurance and another one for 'benefits' since he thought that a pension and some life assurance ought to start off straight away. He allowed 7.5% of salary for the pension and life assurance. Next, he looked at all of his operating costs (ranging from rent to business travel) and estimated monthly costs for each item.

Looking at his Capital Expenditure (CapEx), John costed out what it would take to set up an office (table, chair, filing cabinets etc plus a simple phone/FAX machine) together with computing costs. That surprised him — some £13,875 in total for the first month. Added to the £6,892 of OpEx for the first month (plus another £500 contingency) he saw that he'd need £21,267 in the first month alone. Which was a problem: he only had £10,000 of savings to kick off the business. Before going to see his bank manager about a loan however, John looked at what realistic income he could expect and plugged those details into the spreadsheet. What that showed him was that if he borrowed £10,000 from the bank he should be able to pay that off in the first year of trading (and hence save some loan interest) and, with a bit of luck, be able to pay himself back the £10,000 of savings as well.

Armed with this information, John thought that he should meet with his bank manager and discuss the proposal so he printed off the business plan and the cash flow forecasts but took his portable pc with him, "just in case". The bank manager liked the fact that John was putting in the same amount of cash as requested from the bank and that the business plan was sound and the cash flow estimates sensible. However, the bank manager pointed out that despite earning £99,800 over the first year against costs of £98,735 John would need an overdraft facility of £5,000.

This surprised John, to say the least, so the bank manager added another line at the bottom of the spreadsheet, labelled "Monthly bank balance" and sure enough, he saw that he would be overdrawn for seven months of the year and close to £5,000 overdrawn for March, April and May. He also saw that the bank balance at the end of the year matched the difference between "cash in" and "cash out" for the year. Which was reassuring at least.

Feeling shame-faced, and regretting not having talked with his accountant first, John nevertheless felt that the bank manager was genuinely trying to be helpful. In the following discussion it was decided that the bank would loan John the £10,000 and that this could be paid off over a ten-month period and, further, that a £5,000 overdraft would be put in place. The bank manager asked John to give him updates every month by telephone and to come in for a chat if anything changed. The bank also required various forms of security from John but we won't bore you with those details.

CASE STUDY: MANCHFORD MACHINERY MANUFACTURING (MMM)

John Harcourt's predicted turnover (cash in) was £99,800 but that of MMM is predicted to be considerably more. But you'd expect that for a bigger business. Incidentally, note that whilst John's total cash in was nearly £100,000 he only paid himself a salary of £26,000. So be aware that you can't go paying yourself huge salaries to start with! Anyway, back to MMM — there's a bit of a story here. The initial discussion at the bank was, overall, very positive. The bank manager was impressed with the market research that the team had done and with the business plan overall.

However, she felt that despite the partners putting into the business a loan of £120,000 (from redundancy payouts and savings) she could not offer more than £80,000 over five years as a bank business loan. This would have been OK but the cash flow forecast suggested that by June of the first year the overdraft would therefore rise to nearly £40,000 even though the business bank account was projected to be in credit by the year end.

With the loan of £80,000 the bank manager felt that an additional £40,000 overdraft was an unacceptable "lending exposure" for the bank and that she could offer a maximum overdraft facility of £15,000 such that, together with the business loan of £80,000, the bank's lending exposure was kept below £100,000 in total. This posed the partners with a bit of a problem; well a problem to the tune of £25,000 to be precise. The partners had already done all they could to get the £120,000 together in the first place. However, David Petworth was able to get a short-term loan of £25,000 from his sister but with two conditions; she would like it paid back within one year and she would like £5,000 on top ie £30,000. The partners decided that this was acceptable, given the risk that David's sister was taking and so agreed.

With that additional £25,000 "plugged in", the spreadsheet showed that the maximum overdraft would be under £15,000 even at its worst in June of that year. The best solution was to pay David's sister £10,000 per month for September, October and November of that year — the numbers all added up. Back to the bank…

The bank manager looked again at the spreadsheet and was comfortable with the new short-term loan arrangement. However, she grilled the partners about the £120,000 that they were putting into the business. "Did they", she asked, "intend to repay that loan to themselves before they had repaid the bank loan?" They indicated that they would wish to do so. She frowned a bit and said, "So you are asking the bank to take more risk that you intend to take?" In the discussion that followed it was agreed that, since the partners intended to pay themselves less than they might have expected from employment elsewhere, it seemed fair that they repaid from the business the loan that they had put in month by month. The bank manager did advise them not to take money out of the business too rapidly and so it was agreed that the repayments to themselves would be 'capped' at £6,000 per month and would not start until the short-term loan had been repaid to David's sister.

Each of the partners had to provide additional security to the bank regarding the £80,000 business loan, which essentially meant security over their houses. Since David's sister had asked for no security at all, they left the meeting feeling that paying her £5,000 for taking the risk was actually quite fair.

It was agreed that the partners could therefore start off their business but the bank manager requested that they provide monthly cash flow statements and that if cash flow varied by more than 10% from the budget in any one month that they meet with her to review matters.

HOMEWORK TIME

Now is the time to start building your own cash flow forecast for your business. The best approach is to begin by collecting all of the information that you can be reasonably confident about — such things as:

* what you intend to pay yourself and any employees

* what the insurance costs will be

* costs for renting premises

* lease costs for vehicles or major items of equipment

When you have collated all of the information about the costs associated with running your business, you can then work out how much money you will need to generate from sales in order to make a profit. That information can also be used to help you set prices for your products and services. Of course the price that you set will also be influenced by how many sales you can make over the year. Remember that you may not sell much in the first few months of trading.

Realistically, you will probably find that your business will need start-up funding (to cover initial start-up costs) and it is vital to know how much that will be. Many businesses fail because they are under-funded from the outset. You may also have "ups and downs" over the year if there is a seasonal aspect to your business. This may argue for having an overdraft facility in place.

Once you have a draft cash flow forecast, visit your accountant to discuss this overall budget and the best forms of finance that you might require.

Of all the chapters in this book, this one should be the most
exciting and, perhaps, the most important one. OK... you may
be substituting "daunting" for "exciting" but do remember
that your business plan will define your goals, for perhaps the next three to
five years, and what you will need to do to achieve them. Big stuff really.

If used correctly, the business plan that you are about to produce should be
the document that you return to, again and again, over the coming years. It is
important not to think of this plan as a "static" document but rather a "living"
one that will evolve as your business develops and/or responds to change.

GETTING DOWN TO WRITING THE PLAN

Here's our view on the business plan structure:

1 Executive summary   *(1 page only)*

2 Introduction   *(approx 8 pages)*
      2.1   Introduction to the business
      2.2   Technology review (if appropriate)
      2.3   Intellectual property
      2.4   Licensing

3 Business Opportunity   *(approx 10 pages)*
      3.1   Market description
      3.2   Target Products
      3.3   Competition
      3.4   Commercial strategy
      3.5   Market potential

4 Management   *(approx 2 pages)*
      4.1   Directors, partners or owner(s)
      4.2   Key managers
      4.3   Consultants

5 Operating Plan   *(approx 8 pages)*
      5.1   Production (or R&D) plans
      5.2   Corporate alliances
      5.3   Resource requirements
      5.4   Financial analysis

6 Appendices   *(be restrained!)*
      6.1   Relevant reviews
      6.2   Intellectual property
      6.3   Short-form CVs
      6.4   Production or R&D plans
      6.5   Financial projections

Having read the preceding chapters it is likely that you have generated many pages of text — some of it in note form and probably quite a bit printed from web pages as part of your market research. You'll undoubtedly have lots of information to put together into a coherent plan for your business. It can be very daunting trying to get started with sorting all of that out so let's look at a logical approach.

THE FRONT COVER

Many business plans just have a very plain front cover.   No pictures. No colour. No thought about design. Some people use the word "dull" to describe that kind of approach. Of course we wouldn't be so rude. Well, OK then… in fact we are very rude about them. But, we think, with good reason. First, if your business plan is going to be sent to a potential investor or your bank manager (as part of a loan request) then it needs to look professional. And secondly, people like investors receive many business plans to read and, the truth is, they don't have time to read them all. Your plan needs to catch their attention — if the front cover looks dull then the chances are that what lies inside may be even duller… would you be keen to read a document like that?

FRONT COVER GRAPHICS

It's no surprise that newspapers use striking images on their front pages. A picture may well "convey a thousand words" but a lack of one conveys just one word… boring. We suggest that you choose an image that has some relevance to your business. "Copyright-free" graphics can be obtained by purchasing a CD or by downloading from the internet. Remember that whilst you can freely use these images so can everyone else. That means that it would be hard to register a design as your own. You could have an artist draw an image for you (like we did for Business Boffins "Reg" logo — Reg is the name of the chap with the big glasses by the way) but expect to pay a few hundred pounds for that. And don't forget that the artist will need to agree in writing that you own all of the rights to the drawing.

The background image can convey a visual representation of what the business is about — this can be very helpful when the business name does not! Choose a bold typeface and a large font size for your business name text. Using WORD, it's a good trick to have the background image in grey with bold text in another colour over the top like we have done. Experiment and have fun!

Remember that your business plan contains highly confidential information about what you intend to be doing over the next one, three or sometimes five years. You don't want anybody simply reading your plan. And you especially don't want it read by a competitor. So keep a log of whom you issue a copy to and release one only under a Confidential Disclosure Agreement (see chapter five, "Protecting your ideas") if at all possible. And business plans should never be photocopied.

THE CONTENTS PAGE

Keep this simple. You are writing a 30-page business plan, not a textbook. This is the first page that you will need to adopt (and stick with) some kind of 'house-style' for your documents. What typeface are you going to choose? We like Verdana. Many people use Times New Roman or Arial but the choice is up to you. On the whole though, make sure it is clear and easy to read since not everyone has perfect eyesight even if you have.

We find that 14-point bold works well for headings with 12 point bold for sub-headings and 12 point for all other text. Be restrained with italics within text otherwise the intended emphasis gets lost. Adopt a format and then stick to it. Don't mix numbered headings with lettered headings - for example:

2   Technology Overview

2.1   Introduction

2.1 (a) Background

much better to use...

2.1.1   Background

If you really *must* have a mission statement then the contents page is a good place to locate it. Having such a small space restrains you from writing too much — ideally it's best to have just one sentence that simply states what the business is all about. People either love them or hate them (we're in the latter camp) but they certainly do focus the mind and help capture the essential nature of the business in a short sentence. An alternative is to have a punchy, Executive Summary…

SECTION 1 - THE EXECUTIVE SUMMARY

The most important page in the business plan… and the one that is written last. It is vitally important to spend time getting this summary right. Financiers are inundated with business plans and a poor Executive Summary is the best way of ensuring that an investor reads no further. First of all, this is a **one-page** summary (have we mentioned that?) and that doesn't mean one page written in tiny 8-point text — that's cheating! The acid test here is that if you can't summarise your business proposal down to a single page then you do not understand your business.

Ideally, this one page should read as a complete narrative in itself - like a one-page synopsis that an author would send to a publisher. And it should be simple. And we mean **really** simple. You are not trying to impress the reader with how clever you are but you are trying to convey the essence of your business proposal in a clear and understandable way. Make sure that your summary includes:

- the nature of your product(s) or service(s)

- how it evolved (*ie* brief history)

- what your intellectual property position is (*ie* that you own it) if appropriate

- how you intend to develop your product(s) or service(s)

- what resources you need (*ie* financial, human, facilities *etc*)

- the commercial opportunity that this offers

- an assessment of the competition (*ie* the risk)

And, as with the rest of the document, only state what is truthful and what you really believe is achievable.

This section is intended to provide the reader with an overview of any technology and it should be written assuming **no** prior knowledge on behalf of the reader. For high technology, knowledge-based business plans this is often quite a difficult task. Nevertheless, it is very important to get this introduction right since, if the reader finds it impossible to understand, he or she may well read no further. There are no hard and fast rules but approximately eight pages in total should be adequate for this section.

All well and good, but what would a wedding planner include in this section? Well, for the wedding planner this may be a simple description of how the business would utilise computer databases to access contact details and product information regarding hotels, florists, car hire, dress hire, photographers *etc* in order to put together a complete service for the happy couple. The use of mobile phones and silent pagers (for use in church) could also be explained. A portable personal computer (pc) might be configured to show video clips of previously arranged weddings or to act as a catalogue of products ranging from wedding cake designs through to wedding stationery examples. And what about honeymoon arrangements? Perhaps the portable pc could be linked (via a mobile phone) to the internet to check on flight departure times and so forth at the wedding reception. Or the travel arrangements for the honeymoon could be offered. Perhaps in conjunction with an experienced travel agent?

And so technology and wedding planning wasn't a joke! In today's modern business environment, technology (and especially the new technology of ITC) can be applied to just about any business.

SECTION 2.1 – INTRODUCTION TO THE BUSINESS

A very simple introduction to the business and any associated technology area is required here. You will go into more detail in the next section — this sub-section allows you to introduce some of the basic concepts that will allow a reader with no prior knowledge to grasp the detail in the next section. Avoid the use of technical words here or explain them simply.

SECTION 2.2 – TECHNOLOGY REVIEW

If the technology has a heavy scientific or technical component then this is the place to describe it. If not, simply leave this part out.

SECTION 2.3 – INTELLECTUAL PROPERTY

If you have any technology suitable for patent protection, then you should tabulate the patents that you hold and the filing dates *etc*. If you have patents then these will almost certainly have been submitted by your patent attorney — why not get the attorney to generate a table for you and simply paste it into your Word file?

Of course, the majority of businesses will have no patents; nevertheless, this is the place where you would list any trademarks that you have registered for example. Or what you intend to do about it if not already done. Have you bought a domain name for the internet? For example, we own **www.businessboffins.com**.

You may have special expertise ("know-how") that makes it impossible for others (or perhaps only a few) to replicate your product or service — if so, explain that know-how here.

SECTION 2.4 – LICENSING

Perhaps you are using someone else's technology through some form of licensing agreement. If so, this is the place that you should explain that arrangement. This isn't the place to talk about other forms of arrangements that you may have with other businesses — that comes later in section **5.2 Corporate Alliances**.

SECTION 3 – BUSINESS OPPORTUNITY

This is the section in which you will summarise the findings of your market research. If you have used a third party to prepare some market research data then state here who that company was. It adds weight to your argument if data that you quote come from an independent source. Well…as independent as a company that you are paying can be!

The whole idea of the business plan is to have a logical flow from one section to the next as an unfolding story that helps to keep the reader's attention. This part of the business plan is a good example of that flow:

- You start off in Section 3.1 *(Market description)* by describing the market overall for your product or service.

- Section 3.2 *(Target products)* is where you describe your product(s) or service(s) themselves.

- In Section 3.3 *(Competition)* you look at the competition and make comparisons that address whether what you have for sale is better than, cheaper than or at least as good as what is already on the market.

- Section 3.4 *(Commercial strategy)* describes how you intend to go about selling your product or service.

- Finally, section 3.5 *(Market potential)* summarises your assessment of sales regarding your product or sales. This is an important section since it leads to the 'sales income' line of the cash flow forecast.

SECTION 3.1 – MARKET DESCRIPTION

This section is where you 'set the scene' in describing the potential for your product or service. You should start with an historical review of the market to date — nothing too ambitious, just a couple of paragraphs that show the reader that you have a good grasp of what has gone before. Then progress to a review of the market under the 'five Ps' of marketing that we described in earlier chapters.

SECTION 3.2 – TARGET PRODUCTS

This is a key section. In this section you need to summarise clearly the main features of your product(s) and/or service(s). If possible, insert a photograph or graphic here to help the description. We think that it's a good idea to take a single page to write this section. With a couple of illustrations and some clear text you'll not only have written this section of the business plan but also have drafted a single page 'summary sheet' for use as an advertising 'flier' or 'product sheet' when your business is up and running.

This isn't the place to say why your product or service is better than anyone else's — that comes in section 3.3 (Competition) but you'll certainly want to draw attention to important features that mark you out from the crowd; this is particularly true if you have identified a 'unique selling point (USP)'. But don't waffle.

SECTION 3.3 – COMPETITION

Don't be afraid to list the competition — it shows that there is a market for your service or product. Do try and develop some kind of summary table and place your product in that table. Assess competitors' products and your own in an objective way; what are the honest strengths and weaknesses of what you will offer in comparison to what others will offer? Of course you'll think your product or service is the best. And that may well be true. But make sure that this section is written in as objective a way as possible. Remember that this section is where you might want to discuss with colleagues, friends or family about what they like or dislike about competitor products and your own.

SECTION 3.4 – COMMERCIAL STRATEGY

Having defined your target product(s) and service(s), and the competition, now is the time to describe how you intend to bring the product to market. By all means take advice on this aspect of the business plan. You may need here to say something about such issues as:

- what advertising you are planning

- if you intend to have some kind of 'product launch' when you start

- whether you will sell direct to the public or via a third party

- if you intend to undertake specialised sales; eg mail order or e-commerce

- whether you may enter into an arrangement with another company who offer products or services that are complementary to your own

The commercial strategy is an integral part of the business plan since it defines how you will make sales. Be realistic here and recognise that you may have to do things one after the other rather than all at the same time.

Of course, your commercial strategy will depend heavily on the type of product or service and the current market. That being said, the most important factor is to demonstrate in your plan that *you do have a commercial strategy*.

This may be no more than a marketing campaign that involves, for example, leafleting businesses in your local town. Or it might range through to a national television advertising campaign. Whatever form your commercial strategy and initial marketing campaign will take, it's important to realise that it is an integral part of your business planning. There are several reasons for this but they can be best summarised by the four "P-words" of the **marketing mix**:

- **Product** — offering the right product or service that will be attractive in the marketplace

- **Price** — setting a price that the buyer deems 'worth it' whilst making a profit

- **Place** — ensuring that your product or service is readily available for your customers; perhaps direct sales, mail order, via a third party outlet or even via the internet

- **Promotion** — your product or service will never sell if your potential customers do not know that it exists

We also add a fifth 'P'

- **People** — always remember that, in business, you are dealing with people

Planning out your commercial strategy on the basis of these five "P-words" will give a far greater chance of success for your business. Varying the marketing mix allows you to come up with an overall offering that is tailored to your target customers. This marketing mix may be different for different groups of customers. For example, compare the offering from a book-shop with that of Amazon. In the book-shop, the customer chooses a book from amongst those on offer and makes a purchase. Exactly the same thing happens with Amazon but there is a "convenience" factor that allows the customer to make a purchase online (**Place**). And at a discount (**Price**).

In this section you will be looking at what sales you can realistically hope to achieve. This projection is, of course, crucial for the cash flow forecast since it defines the "sales income". Estimate sales income on a month-by-month basis and be realistic. Remember that sales may not happen quickly at first and that certain months may be "light" — perhaps the August holiday period or the Christmas period.

This exercise can be a very sobering one. We've seen many people find that they need to sell a lot more than expected once operating costs (production, wages, advertising *etc*) have been subtracted in order to make a profit. Don't fool yourself into thinking that sales will be easier if you simply undercut your competitors — customers have brand loyalty and may be prepared to pay more for a brand that they trust rather than a cheaper "newcomer". Think carefully about your pricing then and don't forget to work out what discounts you could offer if a customer wants to buy in large volume or offers a long-term contract that guarantees sales income over a period of time. You must never let these prices fall below the total costs incurred in making the product or offering the service plus all the other costs of running your business. Seems obvious... but so often this causes businesses to go bust. Here is the Business Boffins simplest-ever pricing strategy equation:

Total sales - Total business costs = Profit

If the profit is positive then all is well, if not then the business is not viable. Yes... this seems very simple. Yes... this seems very obvious. But why then do so many new businesses get into difficulty? Usually one of two reasons:

- **over-estimate of sales** (typically a simple over-estimate of sales or a failure to charge enough for the product or service)

- **under-estimate of business costs** (quite simply, a failure to recognise all of the costs that will be incurred in setting up and running a business)

And so this is a key reason to put the effort into writing a sound business plan... **avoid the avoidable!**

With respect to pricing strategy, you generally have three options:

- an hourly rate for your services

- a fixed-price for a particular service

- a fixed-price for a particular product

And on top of these charges may be 'variable' costs such as postage and packing or mileage charges etc.

SETTING HOURLY RATES

To set an hourly rate when you have never done that sort of thing before start by working out what the **total** costs of running the business will be and what you think is an acceptable profit level (perhaps 10% at the low end up to 60% at a more aggressive high end). Work out what the total figure is for the year. Then divide that figure by the number of hours in the working year (we say 48 weeks to cover holidays, 20 working days per month and 7.5 hours per day to give a total of 7200 working hours per year).

Now, if your total business costs for the year (including wages, insurance, office costs, premises rental, computers, phone bills, travel costs, materials, electric bills etc) come to say, £60,000 then adding 20% profit equals £72,000. And so the hourly rate must be £10 per hour to achieve that. This is simply because £72,000 divided by 7,200 hours equals £10 per hour. But, of course, this assumes that you will be earning each and every hour of the 7,200 hours in the business year. Can you guarantee that - surely not! And so it may be prudent to expect that in the first year you may only have paid work for 50% of the year — that immediately means that you'll need to double your hourly rate to meet target and make it £20 per hour.

These are, of course, crude estimates but give the person who says, "I wouldn't know where to start" a place to begin.

FIXED PRICE SERVICES

Now, if you know that a fixed service takes a fixed amount of time then it is possible to calculate a fixed price for that service from the numbers of hours. Let's say that servicing a car usually takes four hours. And let's recognise that fully equipped garages are expensive places to run and operate such that all costs divided by working hours comes out at £55 per hour. Then a four-hour service job could have a fixed price of £220 plus the costs of parts (like spark plugs) and consumables (like anti-freeze). Seems simple enough. Well… it is as long as you know that all such jobs will take exactly four hours. So this type of 'fixed-price' service is OK when you can be pretty sure you won't take longer than you think. In fact, you'll make more profit if you take less time… which is often why some people may be tempted to "cut corners". But, as often as not, jobs can take longer (and sometimes much longer) than you think. This is when businesses can get into trouble. And so be very careful about fixed-price services unless you can very accurately define how long a service will take to perform.

PRICING PRODUCTS

Product pricing is both a science and an art. Not everyone is good at estimating costs and setting prices. At the most simplest, let's say that a business can manufacture 476 of its only product per year. Let's say that the total costs of running the business are £128,000 per year and that a profit of 12% is looked for. This gives a total cost of £143,360. And so the unit cost per product (assuming all are sold in the year) is £143,360/476 = £301.18. Although the business owner might be prepared to compromise a little on the profit margin and set the sale price at £299 in order to bring it under £300… Anyway, what is clear is that unless the business can sell all of the 476 products for £299 then the targets will not be met. And so here is where a contingency might be allowed for - perhaps the business owner recognises that only 80% of the products will be sold in the year? If that were the case then the product price would have to increase since not 476 but 80% of 476 (approximately 381) units would be sold. Hence the price of each of the 381 units would have to be £143,360/381 or £376.27… quite a big difference.

Now, this pricing may seem very simple and, indeed, we have simplified it to the point at which the writers of business textbooks would be choking over their dandelion tea or their port (depending upon the University). However, you need a sensible starting point and that is what we hope to provide.

But even we have to admit that there are other factors that you need to think about in setting a price for a product or a service. In particular, things that you need to buy in order to run your business may go up in price. And don't forget that stock markets may tumble, crude oil (and hence petrol or diesel) costs may go up, the government may put up taxes, the council may increase business rates or local service charges and so on. It's possible to make sensible guesses about these rises, based upon annual inflation over one year, in your cash flow forecast. Many people, in cash flow forecasts, say that everything will be 5% more expensive next year compared to this year — raw materials, wages, the cost of electricity… even dandelion tea and factor that into their estimates. This is by no means a certain way to avoid problems but it's better than ignoring these factors altogether.

So this section on Market Potential has turned out to be a rather dull explanation of how to set the right price for your time or your service or product. Sorry about that. We won't be offended if you want to go and make a coffee or watch East Enders for a bit (I prefer Coronation Street). But since the way in which you estimate how much money your business will generate in sales income has such an important impact upon whether your business is likely to be successful, and hence sustainable, we felt that we should go into a bit of detail. Quite boring but certainly worth digesting. A bit like bran flakes.

Now the good bit. Here's where you get to talk about something really interesting. You. And, of course, anyone else involved with running your business. It's worth at this point reflecting back on the flow of the business plan. Up until now you will have introduced the reader to the product or service and indicated in the last section what the market potential is likely to be. Now is the time to persuade the reader that the management team are capable of bringing the product to market and taking the business forward.

The next section in the business plan deals with the Operating Plan and so this section is not the place to describe what you will do - it's more important here to describe what you have done in the past; in other words, your relevant experience.

SECTION 4.1 – DIRECTORS, PARTNERS OR OWNERS

For **sole traders**, this means giving a short summary of your academic and professional qualifications (if any) and your recent career history. And be succinct. There's little point in going back fifteen years to a Saturday job in a shoe shop if you've been Head of Sales for a big company more recently. Try to put the experience that you describe into context with respect to what you plan to do. Think quite carefully about this; we'd suggest that you write no more than half a page about yourself as a sole trader.

For **partnerships**, try to write a couple of paragraphs about each of the partners. Try to illustrate that the partners have a range of skills and experience between them such that it is a rational step to bring these different people together. Each partner should have a different job title that illustrates his or her area of responsibility. Not all partners may be treated equally (this should be set out in the partnership agreement) and so seniority should also be explained in this section. For example, one partner may be the "boss" or "Managing Partner" who takes responsibility for the business side of things as opposed to operational matters.

For **Limited Companies**, it will be necessary to set out similar descriptions as for partners except that it's traditional to label directors as "Managing Director", "Finance Director", "Commercial Director" and so on. Also note that one person must be Company Secretary — this can be one of the directors but does not have to be. Some businesses now use terms such as "Chief Executive Officer (CEO)" instead of Managing Director. This makes the business sound like a big corporation, which is fine but perhaps a little over the top if there are less than five people in the business! It's also important to list here any "Non-Executive Directors"; these are usually experienced people who join the board as a director but who do not have direct day-to-day management roles.

Perhaps these "non-Execs" only attend for board meetings or for one or two days per week or even per month. Essentially, non-Execs usually bring to the business a wealth of experience that the "Executive" team (those fully employed by the company and responsible for all day-to-day decisions) can refer to for help and advice. Non-Execs often take responsibility for setting the salary levels for Executive Directors. This means that everyone at the board tries to be nice to them. Usually, a board of Directors will elect a Chairman and this is often a non-Executive role although some companies do have an Executive Chairman who takes a strong hand in running the business overall as opposed to just chairing meetings. It's possible to get confused about all of these terms for people on the board so the best thing is to pick a format and stick to it; *ie* use 'xxx Director' or 'xxx Officer' but don't mix both.

Finally, it's entirely up to you how you name people according to sex; some people use Chairman for both men and women whilst others use Chairman or Chairwoman respectively. Others still try and fudge the issue by calling them Chairperson or simply a Chair. Our advice is that you simply respect people and their sensitivities at all times in business. Chairman or Chairwoman seems sensible. Up to you though.

SECTION 4.2 – KEY MANAGERS

Whilst the people 'at the top' like to pretend that they run the business, quite often certain key employees are invaluable in running the business. A bit like Sergeants in the army. Or Sisters on a hospital ward. Since a business that is a sole trader can also employ people, this section can be the same format for all types of business if appropriate. But if you will work on your own, simply leave bit this out.

SECTION 4.3 – CONSULTANTS

All businesses need consultants. And they are especially valuable to the sole trader. So list them here; in particular, make sure that you state your solicitor and your accountant at the very least.

This part of the business plan follows on from the earlier parts that described the product or service and the manager, or management team, that will run the business. In essence, the Operating Plan defines how you will develop your product or service and bring it to market. It will also set out your plans regarding the finance that you will need in order to start and run your business and also the people that you will need to employ.

For a sole trader, it's likely that you will wish to limit spending at the outset and begin selling your product or service as soon as possible. For partnerships, it may be that you have a longer "lead time" devoted to developing the product or service before you get it to market. And for Limited Companies, there may be quite a long period of time before you get a product to market. All of these strategies call for a clear Operating Plan that sets out exactly what you will need to set up and run the business — both financial and human resources.

This is where you will undoubtedly spend quite a bit of time thinking through exactly how you intend to set up and run the business and then defining exactly what you will need. This plan is then placed into context over time such that you can build up a cash flow forecast on a month-by-month basis. Setting up the cash flow forecast is an incredibly important part of the business plan. It will help you as you move forward to take each step at a time but it will also let you monitor if things are going according to plan or whether the plan needs to change. Your accountant, and probably your bank manager, will almost certainly want to review progress against the cash flow forecast with you. So do not be over-optimistic otherwise you will find yourself constantly "underperforming" against targets that were, in any case, unrealistic from the start.

SECTION 5.1 – PRODUCTION OR R&D PLANS

Not all businesses will have a product or a service to sell from day one of operations. Typically, some time will need to be spent in Research and Development (R&D) or in manufacturing before the product or service can come to market.

We think that the following six-point checklist is quite useful for most types of business:

1 What needs to be done for any product in development and what are the milestones along the way?

2 What needs to be done for any product in manufacture and what are the milestones along the way?

3 What people will you need in order to do all of the work?

4 What facilities/equipment will you need as you progress through the milestones?

5 How much of the work will be contracted out to third parties and who will be the contractors?

6 How much will all of this cost?

Items one to six will vary in relevance to your business plan since each business will be unique. For example, a sole trader business may spend little time on items 1 and 2 since the service being sold comes out of the head of the owner-manager, *ie* that person sells experience and knowledge which are 'products' already in place. However, items 3–6 are all relevant. For a partnership business or a limited company, on the other hand, items 1 and 2 are very important. We feel that this simple six-point checklist is valid for most forms of business.

SECTION 5.2 – CORPORATE ALLIANCES

This section simply details those businesses that (i) you have either entered into some form of contractual arrangement with or, (ii) those that you intend to do so at a later date. We are not thinking here about the company where you buy stationery from every month but rather those key businesses from which you might source vital raw materials. Look at what you will need to purchase in order to run your business — would your business suffer badly if that supplier ceased to supply you? If so, then you need plans in place to ensure a constant supply, which might be some special arrangement with that business, or it might mean that you source essential supplies from more than one business.

Alternatively, you may enter into arrangements with other businesses that will help you find customers; perhaps the arrangement might include paying that other business some percentage of your sales (a 'royalty' payment). Or perhaps you may have an arrangement whereby another business passes work to you when they are too busy to cope. And you might let another business sell your product to their customers having bought it from you at some kind of discount price. These are the sorts of arrangement that need to be detailed in this section.

SECTION 5.3 – RESOURCE REQUIREMENTS

For many people, and especially your bank manager, this will be a key part of the business plan. You have set out your product or service and estimated the market potential. You have said why the manager(s) are the right people to make a go of the business. And you have set out your operating plans. Now is the time to define what this will all cost in terms of people and cash. Remember that there are two forms of expenditure to be thinking about and they can generally be defined as:

Capital Expenditure (CapEx) which are all payments for something that you will own after paying for it such as a workshop machine or the building that you work from (should you purchase rather than rent it).

Operating Expenditure (OpEx) which includes all payments for goods or services that you have received and so includes phone bills, wages bills, stationery items and so on.

One expenditure item that comes under OpEx is the wages bill. For the sole trader, this may mean just one salary whereas it may be for many employees in a limited company. And remember it would be very unusual for all employees to start on the same day; employees tend to be hired as needed and so you will need to develop a "hiring strategy" that defines the sort of person (a job specification) for each employee and that point in time when they will need to be hired. Now remember that this section of the plan is a narrative part — in other words you are describing your operating plan in terms of what you will be doing rather than summarising the costs of all of that into financial tables. The financial summary comes in the next section.

At the outset, coming up with spreadsheets that set out a financial analysis for your new business, looking out for at least one year and perhaps three or five years, seems a scary task to undertake. However, with all of the work that you have done to get to here, this part of the business plan should be comparatively simple to produce.

Full details of the budget, on a month-by-month basis should be prepared as spreadsheets and included in Appendix 6.5. The sequence is as follows:

- **develop the operating plans** (what you intend to do)

- **work out the headcount needs on a month-by-month basis** (who you will need)

- **work out the monthly 'consumables' costs associated with the plans** (what 'operating' expenses you will have)

- **define facility and equipment needs, again referenced to each month** (what 'capital' expenses you will have)

- **cost out any external contracts on a monthly basis** (what you will need to pay for others working on your behalf)

- **predict what sales you will realistically achieve on a month-by-month basis**

From these spreadsheets you can then move forward be to prepare some summaries as follows:

- **hiring strategy**

- **overall Operating Expenditure**

- **overall Capital Expenditure**

- **overall External Contract costs**

- **sales estimates**

- **an overall Cash Flow Forecast**

These spreadsheets go into the Appendices and so a simple 'cash flow' table may be all that is required in section 5.4. Our view is that you could develop the special forms of accounting summaries known as 'Balance Sheets' and 'Profit and Loss Accounts' but that the critical summary is the cash flow forecast. It would, in our view, be very sensible to ask your accountant to develop these other summaries once he or she has checked your business plan and (most likely) amended your cash flow forecasts. Don't be afraid of this review by the accountant — this is not a school exam! In fact, the accountant will almost certainly be able to offer help and advice that will save you money.

SECTION 6 – APPENDICES

Anything that can be 'pruned' out of the business plan (without losing key information or clarity) should be moved into the appendices. There are no rules about appendices. Except, perhaps, to be restrained.

6.1 RELEVANT REVIEWS

Any relevant review of your area of business might be good to include here. If you've had something published yourself that would be great. But things written by a third party might add useful, and impartial, objectivity.

6.2 INTELLECTUAL PROPERTY

If your business will be based upon any form of intellectual property (eg patents) then here is where you should give full details of patent abstracts, trade mark details, territories covered *etc*.

6.3 SHORT-FORM CVs

And we really mean short. For some kinds of business plan the scientific or industrial track record of an individual might bear further detail above and beyond the brief summary given in section 4. But don't go mad. Try to keep things to no more than a page per person.

6.4 PRODUCTION OR R&D PLANS

The rule here is to have two pages per project or product; one page for the plan and one page for any associated narrative *etc.* Simple diagrams that convey the key details are better than over-complicated plans that nobody can understand.

6.5 FINANCIAL PROJECTIONS

We think that you are the right person to draft the initial cash flow forecast for your business. And we showed you how to do just that in the last chapter. But there are other financial formats that could be included here such as the balance sheet and the profit & loss account. Unless you are familiar with those report formats, we suggest that you ask your accountant to help. In any case, we think that the cash flow forecast is the most important financial projection. The reason we are so keen on cash flow forecasts is that it is a way of setting out what money you expect will come into the business (loans, investment and income from sales) and what money you expect to go out of the business (capital purchases like big equipment or operating expenses like stationery or wages). By preparing a monthly cash flow forecast it is possible to look at **when** as well as **how much** money will move in and out of your business. This can be important when asking the bank manager for an overdraft facility because overdrafts are useful to cover 'blips' in cash flow or to cover a start-up period before income begins to come in.

HOMEWORK TIME...

Now is the time to start putting your own business plan together. Create a Word file and add the various section headings that we recommend — delete any that are not relevant to your own business. Leave the Executive Summary to the end and start with the Introduction (Section 2). Try to work your way through the plan, from start to finish, one section at a time since this helps establish a logical "narrative flow".

You'll almost certainly find it quite a struggle to keep below 30 pages even though that seems a lot when you begin. Writing your business plan is something that will require several versions until you achieve a document that will work. Do get it reviewed by friends and family as feedback at an early stage can be very helpful. Finally, try to avoid having photographs of large file size embedded within your business plan — this can create a Word file so large it becomes impossible to email to people such as your accountant.

First off, assuming that you've written the plan using WORD, don't forget to run the spell-checker function. You'll miss typos when you read it yourself but they suddenly jump off the page when discussing the business plan with your bank manager! Secondly, do have your business plan reviewed by your advisers. We think that the business plan should be reviewed by your accountant. Indeed, your accountant may be required to help you with some of the financial forecasts. And she will be able to advise on the forms of finance that you should seek if you need access to start-up funding. Spending money with an accountant may seem extravagant at the outset but many people say that a good accountant is likely to save you more money with your business than you get charged in fees. And thirdly, remember that the business plan is an evolving document and will require updating and revision.

So that's it. How we think you should approach business planning. We've got more help about financial planning in the chapter that follows. And if you think that the best strategic minds don't have to bother with planning, here's a little history lesson (not at all boring either):

NAPOLEON'S MARCH ON MOSCOW - 1812/13

In the Summer of 1812, Napoleon set off from the Polish border with a force approaching half a million souls heading for Moscow. When he got there, out of the half a million, only 100,000 were still left alive. The campaign was a disaster and he headed back to the Polish border. **_He arrived back with only 10,000 souls._**

Yes, that's right. Close on half a million dead. And did they die as a result of battle? Some did, but most died because of the **cold weather.** *It was simply colder, wetter and took longer than they had planned for.*

So this disaster was **avoidable.** Inadequate planning resulted in half a million souls simply being prepared inadequately for the cold.

Remember that planning for success means removing as much risk as possible: *avoid the avoidable.*

In the last chapter, "Writing your business plan", we showed you how to produce both a business plan and a cash flow forecast. Hopefully you've made some progress with this. The cash flow forecast is particularly relevant to this chapter, as it tells you how much (if any) start-up cash you are going to need. Assuming you do need some start-up cash, the obvious next question is "where will this come from?" Two places that new businesses often turn to for financial support are **banks** and **business angels**.

We are all familiar with banks as a source of finance. They lend money to businesses on the condition that it is paid back at some future date and that certain interest charges are paid along the way. This type of finance is referred to as **debt finance** and usually comes in the form of an overdraft or loan. All business structures — sole traders, partnerships and limited companies — are able to apply for debt finance.

Equity finance only applies to Limited Companies as investors buy shares in the company

Business angels, on the other hand, *invest* money in businesses in exchange for a proportion of its shares (or equity). This type of finance is therefore referred to as **equity finance**. Only limited companies can consider this as a possible route towards raising finance, since only they are capable of issuing shares. Unlike debt finance, equity finance is not something that the new business has to pay back to the investor. In buying shares, the investor buys a share of the business. If that business does well, then those shares may be sold later at a profit, or the investor may take a share of business profits every year in proportion to the number of shares held. If the business fails and becomes worth nothing, then the investor's shares are also worth nothing… in other words, the investment is lost.

Hence business angels are often wealthy people who can afford to lose the money invested in any *one* business but who look to see an overall gain from a *range* of investments — often termed a portfolio of investments.

Let's begin by looking at banks. Pretty obviously, you will need to have a business bank account so that your business can make and receive payments. The bank statement (usually monthly but sometimes weekly or even daily) provides you with a documented account of all cash transactions going into or out of your bank account. This is very useful in preparing your business accounts. As well as providing you with your basic business account, banks provide a range of other services, including insurance, pension plans, international currency exchange and, of course, debt finance. Most banks now offer electronic banking too; this means you can make payments, transfer money and set up direct debits over the internet.

CHOOSING WHO TO BANK WITH

Banks differ widely in terms of what they offer the small business sector, so it pays to shop around between banks and even between different branches of the same bank. Although most businesses choose to bank with one of the 'Big Four' — Barclays, HSBC, LloydsTSB and Royal Bank of Scotland Group (including NatWest) — there are plenty of others out there who are worth considering. Things to be thinking about when choosing a bank include:

- *Location* — is it nearby and easy to get to? If you're going to be making frequent cash deposits, then this will be an important factor.

- *Bank charges* — bank charges are based on the amount of work passing through your account. This may take the form of a fixed amount charged periodically (eg monthly, quarterly), a charge for each item passing through your account, or a charge based on the turnover of your account during the charging period. Charging policies can vary significantly from bank to bank. Many banks offer new businesses free banking for the first year and some follow this with discounting their standard charges for a time.

- *Debt finance charges* — are you intending to borrow money from the bank? If so, then make sure you are clear about what costs (interest and other charges) are associated with it. As with bank charges, there is a great deal of variation between banks. We'll be looking at debt finance in more detail in a moment.

- ***Personal relationship*** — it's important that you find your bank manager easy to get along with and easy to talk to. Some people choose to open a business account at the same bank where they hold their personal account, simply because they know the bank manager and can prove to him or her that they are a creditworthy customer with a good record. Others choose a different bank in order to keep personal and business issues apart.

DEBT FINANCE

Banks are the largest suppliers of debt finance to businesses in the UK. As we said earlier, debt finance usually comes in one of two forms: an *overdraft* or *a loan*.

OVERDRAFTS

An overdraft is the most flexible and simplest form of borrowing available. It provides you with short-term finance, which is ideal for covering the day-to-day costs (predictable) of running your business. It also helps you cope with difficulties arising if your customers are late in settling their debts (unpredictable). Most businesses will request an overdraft facility even if they do not intend to be overdrawn. The reason for this is that it allows you to cope with some of the unpredictable issues like late payment from a customer.

Overdrafts are not appropriate as a source of long-term finance, or to purchase fixed assets (*buildings, motor vehicles etc.*), as they are *repayable upon demand*. In addition, an overdraft facility normally has to be renegotiated every 6–12 months. Interest is payable only on the amount you are overdrawn each day. Some banks also charge an arrangement fee for setting up the overdraft, typically 1%–1.25% of the amount requested. Always speak to your bank to arrange an overdraft rather than risking an unauthorised one.

It is important to be aware of the charges connected with exceeding the agreed overdraft limit – additional interest will be charged, and banks usually charge for informing you of this, too. There are also charges for bounced cheques.

LOANS

A loan is a suitable form of finance for longer-term purchases, such as vehicles or essential business equipment. Loans differ from overdrafts in that they are for a fixed amount and have a fixed repayment schedule. Although the interest rate charged on a loan may be slightly less than on an overdraft, there is no opportunity to vary the amount of financing, and interest is payable on the full amount of the outstanding loan. However, on the positive side, once a loan has been arranged, the financing is secure for the life of the loan (unless, of course, you fail to make the necessary repayments or break any of the clauses in the loan contract). The bank may insist that you take out some form of 'payment insurance' (usually one of their own products!) to protect against you being unable to make the repayments.

THE BANKER'S PERSPECTIVE

Getting your bank manager to agree to an overdraft or loan is not straightforward. Bank lending decisions are traditionally based around the CAMPARI model. More are moving towards automated lending decisions but the CAMPARI model will show you the kind of questions your bank may ask before making a decision:

Character — are you trustworthy and do you have a good credit history?

Ability — are you capable of achieving what the business plan proposes? Have you carried out market research? How good is your product? Do you have the necessary experience?

Margin — how risky is your proposal and what interest rate would reflect this risk? Remember, the bank doesn't really share in your success but it does suffer if your venture fails.

Purpose — what is the purpose of the overdraft/loan and its relevance to your business? Does the demand for the product or service justify the investment?

Amount — does the amount seem too little or too much? How much are you putting in to the business yourself? How have you worked out the amount you're asking for?

Repayment — are you able to generate enough money to repay the overdraft/loan and interest?

Insurance — is there a contingency plan for repaying if things don't work out as expected? Can you provide any security against the overdraft/loan?

Your bank may in principle agree to offer you a loan but certain issues will need to be resolved before you can draw down the money. The key ones are:

- *Interest rate* — the interest rate charged by banks can be fixed, variable (a number of percentage points over the bank base rate), or at a monthly managed rate and should be agreed at the outset. Typically a variable interest rate may be between 3% to 7% over the bank base rate. Banks will set interest rates only after they have evaluated the risk involved in lending you the money, looked at what stake you have in the business (the more you have, the lower the interest rate), and considered the security you have provided them. Look out for the APR (annual percentage rate) – generally, the lower this is, the cheaper the loan or overdraft will be.

- *Repayment schedule (for loans)* — with a loan you will need to negotiate how and when the repayments should be made. There may be various options open to you. For example, you might be able to negotiate an initial 'holiday' period whilst income is still building up. Also, check to see if there are any penalties if you repay the loan early.

- *Security* — in all probability your bank will want you to pledge business or personal assets as security against the loan you're asking for. The most common types of security banks seek are a mortgage over business premises or a debenture (this gives the bank a mortgage over all the assets of the business including the book debts; however it can only be applied to a limited company or a farmer). If you cannot offer sufficient security from the assets of your business, the bank may ask for personal assets such as personal guarantees from the directors of the company or a mortgage over private property. If you are still not able to provide adequate security, you should consider finance under the Government's "Small Firms Loan Guarantee Scheme". As well as asking for security, banks generally attach various terms and conditions (or covenants) to granting loans, which must be complied with throughout the term of the loan. Always seek advice from your solicitor before providing security or covenants on a loan.

The Small Firms Loan Guarantee Scheme is a Department of Trade and Industry (DTI) initiative that guarantees loans from banks and other financial institutions for small businesses that have viable business proposals but who have tried and failed to get a conventional loan because of a lack of security. More than 20 banks now participate in the scheme. A complete list of the lenders involved is available on the Business Link website — go to **www.businesslink.gov.uk**.

Loans of up to £250,000 are available for periods of between 2 and 10 years. The SFLG scheme will underwrite 75% of the loan. In return for the guarantee the borrower pays the SFLG scheme a premium of 2% per year on the outstanding amount of the loan as well as interest to the lender. Many business activities are eligible but there are several exclusions and some restrictions do apply. You can get further information from the Business Link website (see above). Remember that schemes like this change frequently so check before building into your business plan!

BUSINESS ANGELS

As we mentioned earlier, business angels are wealthy individuals (or groups of individuals working together) who invest money in businesses in return for a proportion of its shares. Therefore it is only **limited companies** that can consider this as a means of raising finance.

Selling shares in your business means you will lose some of the potential gains you might make as a result of the shares increasing in value over time. But this, of course, is the great attraction for the investor. Most business angels will only consider investing in a new company if the expected average return (in terms of the increase in share value) is at least 20%–30% per year. Unless you can offer them this, they are unlikely to invest. A typical business angel investment, from one individual, could be anything between £10,000 and £250,000. Finance needs up to £2million could be made up from a group of business angels but equity finance over £2million is usually provided by venture capital firms rather than business angels. The exceptions are when several business angels invest together in a syndicate or when they co-invest alongside venture capital funds.

If you are considering raising finance through investment from one or more business angels, then you have to be willing to develop a personal relationship with them. Typically, they may want hands-on involvement with your business after they have made an investment. Of course, this can be a good thing as business angels often have a great deal of commercial experience, which you can dip in to, and their involvement may make it easier for you to attract additional finance. However, some people are very protective about their own business and dislike the thought of any outsiders getting involved. If you think you fall into this category, then raising finance through business angels is probably not the right option for you.

Getting a business angel to invest in your business is not easy. You need to have a strong and credible business plan and the ability to present the investment opportunity in a convincing manner. But first, of course, you need to find a business angel to approach.

FINDING A BUSINESS ANGEL

Business angels can be hard to find because they're often busy with their own businesses. However, there are a number of ways you can go about finding one:

- **Informal contact**

- **Professional advisers**

- **Introduction agencies (including "business angel networks")**

Many contacts with business angels are made **informally.** Do you know of any wealthy businessmen or women who live in your area? If so, you might conveniently arrange to bump in to them at a local business event. Remember that business angels tend to invest locally, so we would suggest starting your search within a 50-mile radius of your business premises.

Professional advisers, and in particular accountants, are likely to know of business angels who are active in your area. Assuming you have a good working relationship with them, they might be able to put a good word in for you, too. It's also worth asking your bank manager if he or she is aware of any.

Many of the most active business angels use the services of **introduction agencies** to find out about interesting investment opportunities. In order to register with one of these agencies, you will usually have to supply your business plan and financial forecasts. Once you are registered, the agency will pass your information on to the business angels registered with it. Typically, they will be invited to attend meetings where you (along with a few other businesses) are given the opportunity to present to them. A guide to these agencies can be found at the British Venture Capital Association website (www.bvca.co.uk). The guide lists contact names, geographical area, fees payable, registration criteria, methods of matching *etc.*

One last point: you should allow yourself plenty of time to find the right business angel. **It may take six months to find someone suitable (and a further three months to agree a deal).**

PRESENTING TO A BUSINESS ANGEL

Having found a suitable business angel to approach, you now need to show them why they should invest in your business. You don't usually get much time or space to present to them, so you need to be concise and convincing. Think of it as the biggest sales pitch you will ever make … for that is probably what it will be. In the next chapter, "Raising finance" we look in more detail at the components of a funding presentation. Always keep in mind what the investor is looking for when you prepare your presentation. They will want to see:

- that you have a product or service offering a unique selling proposition and addressing the needs of a large and growing market

- that you are offering them a potentially highly profitable opportunity

- that you have a management team with expertise, experience and drive

- that you will use the money they give you in a sensible and effective manner

- that you are "someone they can work with"

Investments by business angels are comparatively informal and rely on a greater deal of personal chemistry and trust than other forms of financing. Although they will want to see a thorough business plan, they are more likely to act on a hunch rather than relying on complex appraisal (or "due diligence" as it is termed in the trade).

Once a business angel has expressed an interest in investing in your business, you need to establish that they can provide the level of financing that you require. Of course, if you are looking to raise a large amount of money, then you may need to approach more than one investor. But you do not want to waste time with someone who has insufficient funds. Negotiating a deal with a business angel can be a lengthy and complicated process. Here's a rundown of some of the key issues that you will probably discuss:

- **Share price** — the value you consider your company's shares to be worth might be different to what an investor thinks they're worth. Obviously, the higher the share price, the less of your company you will have to "give away" for a given investment. ***NB Setting a price for shares in a company requires professional advice.***

- **Salaries and dividends** — what salaries, fees and dividends will be paid to you, the management team? And under what circumstances can these be changed?

- **Exit strategy** — a business angel will at some stage want to sell their shares in order to cash in on their (hopefully) increased value. They will want to know how and when they will be able to do this (eg through a trade sale, flotation on the stock market *etc* in *circa* 'x' years time).

- **Responsibilities** — if the business angel is going to be involved with the business, what responsibilities will they have?

- **Legal issues** — the business angel may ask you to provide a warranty confirming that information you have provided is true. If the business fails later and it can be proved that you gave misleading information, the investor will usually have the right to compensation. You may also be asked to provide indemnities, where you agree to accept liability in certain circumstances eg if the company is sued in relation to contracts which have already been agreed. **Get advice from your solicitor on this matter.**

Before handing over the cash, a business angel will probably want to check your company's financial and legal details, and confirm other points about your business and market. Or rather, they will instruct their own legal and financial team to do so on their behalf.

They may also provide an external 'expert' with details of your business for an expert assessment; this is particularly true for businesses that are based on some form of new technology. Your accountant will be able to help you prepare any financial information you need and should be able to advise you on what form the investment should take. For example, it may be possible to structure it to make it more tax efficient for the business angel. Your solicitor will need to be involved with the preparation of the Shareholders' Agreement; this document will define certain rights of shareholders such as their ability to sell or transfer shares.

CONCLUSIONS

Banks and business angels offer two contrasting methods of raising finance. Whether you choose to borrow money in the form of an overdraft or loan, or issue shares in exchange for an investment (or both) depends on the structure of your business and what the money is being used for.

In general:

- for development costs and to finance start-up losses, equity (investment) finance may be the best bet although this is only available for limited companies

- for equipment and vehicles, a fixed term loan is often the most appropriate solution (unless you elect to use some form of lease finance)

- for short-term working capital, an overdraft may offer the solution

A final point about banks. Don't treat your bank the way most people treat their dentist, only going to them if you have toothache. Asking for help when problems first appear, rather than when they accumulate into a crisis, will probably prompt a more positive response and will maintain your reputation as an excellent customer.

This reputation may be crucial if a real crisis emerges that threatens the survival of your business — the bank's attitude might then be critical.

Effective financing is not an easy process and there are various mechanisms to be considered, as we saw in the last chapter. In setting about raising funds for real, it seems only fair to warn you that there may be disappointments along the way. For example, one bank manager may not wish to make you a business loan or one investor may not wish to buy shares in your company. Don't give up! If you get rejections then try and find out why you were rejected. Can you learn anything and improve your plan before trying again? However, there are certain things that you can do to improve your chances of success and so this chapter attempts to summarise some of those.

WHAT MONEY DO YOU NEED?

The first question to ask, irrespective of your business structure, is "What money do you need?" The reason for this is that you should raise finance according to need — never raise business finance and then think how to spend it! In writing your business plan we asked you to create a cash flow spreadsheet; the process was to look at all of your costs (both set-up and ongoing) over the first year (and perhaps, later years too) and then to make a realistic estimate of income. Any shortfall between the two gives a simple estimate of what finance you will need. And remember that the finance may be a mixture of cash when you start the business and an overdraft facility as the business moves forward. Let's start with the simplest form of business finance — business banking.

> The key to start-up finance is to raise the money that you need – neither less nor more

BUSINESS BANKING

Typically, a sole trader would expect to make sales in the first year of operation. Usually then, a sole trader may require capital to start the business off and then an overdraft facility to cover business costs along the way. Start-up capital and overdrafts are interlinked since both would represent components of the same 'lending decision' that a bank manager would have to make.

A business loan could offer you, for example, £10,000 at the beginning to be paid off (with interest) over a five-year period. Interest rates vary but let's say that the repayment amount was £225 per month with an additional £25 per month insurance payment protection premium that your bank manager might insist that you take out. That would give a monthly repayment of £250 spread over 60 months — or £15,000 in total. Hence, whilst you borrow £10,000 the overall cost to the business will be £15,000, *ie* a cost of £5,000. This may seem like a lot but you have to remember that this could make the difference as to whether you are able to start in business or not. And, if the business is more successful than you predict, the loan could be paid off sooner with a saving in overall interest charged (do check with your bank manager about any penalty charges for early repayment of loans).

In looking at your application for a business loan, the bank manager will want to review your business plan and your cash flow forecast along the lines of the CAMPARI model that we discussed in the last chapter. There are key questions to be answered:

- Are both the business idea and the business plan sound?

- Is the cash flow forecast comprehensive and are the sales projections realistic?

- Can the business support the costs of the business loan?

- And perhaps most importantly… are you, in the bank manager's judgement, capable of running the business?

These questions are usually answered during a discussion in the bank manager's office. But there may be other questions that the bank will wish to address:

- Have you kept your personal finances in order during your time with the bank?

- What are your borrowings elsewhere (*eg* mortgage repayments, credit cards etc) and will income that you propose to take from the business cover those costs?

- What risk are you taking?

Now it may seem odd that the bank manager will want to see you take a risk. And by risk here we mean what money you are putting into the business to start it up or whether you offer your house as security against a business loan. By taking a risk with assets of your own you are telling your bank manager that you really believe in the business idea (and in your own capability of making a success) and so you should inspire confidence.

As a sole trader, your bank manager may also wish to meet your partner (if you have one), especially if you intend to employ them even on a part-time basis. This will be true in those situations when assets that you own jointly with your partner (such as a house) are used as security for a business loan. Remember that the bank manager will be selling you a **product.** Both business loans (plus any associated insurance from the bank) and the interest on any overdraft are products that the bank sells to you. So you need to shop around. Talk with several different banks. But remember that the bank where you have your personal account may be your best bet simply because they know you. However, business banking is a competitive arena these days so it is certainly worth looking around.

A key issue is to decide what component of lending is sensible to take out as a business loan and what as an overdraft facility. On the whole, banks will want overdraft facilities to be kept to a minimum. However, let's say in our example that your cash flow forecast predicts a deficit over year one as follows:

Month	Deficit	With £10,000 loan
January	−£14,456	−£4,456
February	−£12,216	−£2,216
March	−£13,487	−£3,487
April	−£14,124	−£4,124
May	−£13,953	−£3,953
June	−£12,376	−£2,376
July	−£11,923	−£1,923
August	−£12,198	−£2,198
September	−£11,263	−£1,263
October	−£10,830	−£830
November	−£9,250	+£750
December	−£8,600	+£1,400

In this example, with the £10,000 loan the business account is never overdrawn by more than £5,000 and the account is in credit for the last two months of the year. In this situation, the bank manager may be prepared to offer you the £10,000 business loan plus a £5,000 overdraft facility with the proviso that the overdraft is only for a 12-month period. This would seem a sensible arrangement.

If the cash flow forecasts for subsequent years show that the business account continues to build up a positive credit then it would be sensible to ask about early repayment options for the business loan. However, cash flow is always a problem for small businesses — your forecast will assume that all of your customers will pay on time… many do not! So don't be in too big a hurry to repay loans unless you are confident that things are, and will continue, going well. Also, ensure that you have enough money to start the business and to run it — many businesses fail in the early years because they are under-funded, not because the business is a bad idea.

Now this is a simple example but it does illustrate how to come up with a sensible proposal for your bank manager. But there are other considerations. For example, how much do you put in yourself and how much should you ask the bank manager for? In simplistic terms, it may be a good rule of thumb to try and illustrate to the bank manager that you are risking as much as he or she is. So in order to borrow £10,000, can you illustrate that you are putting in the same amount? This does not mean cash — look at the following list:

Computer system	£3,500
Office furniture	£1,200
Cash	£5,300

This list totals £10,000 but only £5,300 represents cash from yourself — the rest is composed of your assets that you are putting into the business, *ie* things that you have already paid for. Of course, the bank manager will point out that the bank is also taking a risk over the £5,000 overdraft facility as well…

Now few people will be in the position that they can put in substantial funds to start a business at the outset such that they don't need a bank loan. Some use a redundancy payout to help start their business of course but most have to rely on savings. And in today's world, most of us find it a struggle to save much. So, quite often, people will look to borrow some money from friends and/or family.

You must make absolutely sure that friends and family clearly understand your business idea and that there will be risks associated with lending money. You need a written agreement for anyone who lends you money — this should be drawn up by a lawyer. The agreement should clearly state what the terms are relating to the loan including the repayment schedule and any interest to be paid. The document should also describe what will happen in the event that your business fails — will the friend or relative look to you to still pay back the loan? The presumed answer is yes! In general, we would urge caution about borrowing money from friends and family unless it is done in a very professional way such that there are no misunderstandings about the risk.

Banks, of course, make lending facilities available to a range of businesses — from sole trader to limited companies. Loans may be from a few thousand to many millions depending upon the size of the business. Although in our previous example we referred to an individual as a sole trader, the principles of business banking remain very similar irrespective of business structure. Perhaps one clear difference between a sole trader and a limited company is that the law considers the limited company to be an entity in its own right; for the bank this may mean that whilst the 'company' takes out a loan the bank may still require security and guarantees from the directors of the company or other parties willing to 'underwrite' the loan, *ie* take the risk away from the bank. For most limited companies however, raising finance is done via the equity finance route, *ie* selling shares.

EQUITY FINANCE — THE HKM CASE STUDY

In contrast to borrowing via some form of business loan or overdraft facility, limited companies have the option to raise finance by the selling of shares in the company. Since this book is geared towards small businesses (and micro-businesses with less that 10 employees in particular) it is unlikely that you will be raising millions of pounds to begin with. Let's take an example:

Perhaps **Hillside Kitchen Manufacturers Ltd (HKM)** wishes to purchase manufacturing equipment costing £250,000 and that costs over the first year amount to another £250,000; a total of £500,000 altogether.

In this situation, the first question to answer is whether it is sensible to purchase the manufacturing equipment outright or whether HKM could lease the equipment. This may cost HKM more in the long run but it would limit the amount of money raised by selling shares, termed 'equity release'. Perhaps raising £300,000 would be adequate if it covered the £250,000 of running costs plus an extra £50,000 to cover leasing costs for year one? Why would HKM wish to limit the amount of shares sold? Quite simple really: *the bigger a portion of the company that you sell then the less you will own.* And so ultimately your own share of profits from the company once trading, or the proceeds of any future trade sale (should the company be sold) will be reduced. So the trick is to raise as much money as possible for the fewest number of shares… easier said than done!

Anyway, back to HKM. In order to raise equity finance, HKM will have to sell shares to the value of the money that is needed — in this case £300,000. The process of raising equity finance can be simply described as follows:

- define how much money will be required to fund the period of time in question

- define the current value of the company and hence set a price per share (company value divided by number of shares)

- sell shares to the value of the cash needed

Now this is all very well so long as the company has a high value such that only a limited number of shares need to be sold in order to raise the required funds. For a new company like HKM this is unlikely to be the case. Let's say that HKM wanted to raise the £300,000 but only wanted to release one third of their shares for sale — how would they do this? Well, assuming that there are 100,000 shares already issued and in the hands of the founders of the company then they could issue another 50,000 new shares and sell them for £300,000. There would therefore be 150,000 shares in total such that the 50,000 sold for cash represent 33.3% of the business. And each of those 50,000 shares would be sold for £6 such that £300,000 of equity finance would be raised. But hang on a minute. Doesn't that mean that every share is worth £6? Yes it does. So that means the shares owned by the founders, the original 100,000, are all worth £6 each? Yes it does. So doesn't that mean that the company valuation was 100,000 x £6 or £600,000 before any cash was raised? Yes it does. And that the company is worth £900,000 after cash? Yes it is… Blimey!

How on earth could the founders claim a value of £600,000 when they started their business? Well… on the face of it this does seem mighty cheeky. But perhaps the founders had taken out some patents that covered a new manufacturing process for coating kitchen units with a new material that was heat and stain resistant and gave a much working longer life? Then the value of the business would lie in their *intellectual* property and so a valuation for the business could be determined from predicted sales and profit in later years.

CAUTION !

Don't try this at home! Making determinations of company value (and hence share price) is both a science and an art — make sure that you get advice from your accountant.

Please take note of this caution. Setting a value for your company and hence being able to set a share price is something that you will have to be able to defend vigorously with any potential investor — **you must take professional advice.** On the one hand, you may set the price too low and hence give away a bigger proportion of your company than you need to do. On the other hand, you may set the share price too high in which case investors will not be interested.

The whole issue of setting a share price is one that requires expert handling. Many companies recognise that their value may be low to start with but that it will increase substantially as time goes on as the company makes significant progress. Hand in hand with this progress will be specific achievements (or 'milestones') that add to the value of the company. Recognising that the company value will progress as time goes on, many companies start out by raising limited funds at the outset but plan for 'second round' and 'third round' funding later. They do this because they can sell shares at the later equity finance rounds for a higher price than that at the start of the company life. Here is an example of a company that raised finance over several rounds… together with the impact that it had on the founders' shareholding:

Round	Shares	Price	Total shares	Founders %
1	60,000	£1	60,000	100%
2	40,000	£8	100,000	60%
3	100,000	£25	200,000	30%
4	300,000	£38	500,000	12%

Let's just go through this round by round:

In the **first round**, the founders set up their business with some of their own capital and issued 60,000 shares at £1 each. This meant that they owned 100% of the business and that the market capitalisation (the value or 'market cap') was £60,000, being the number of shares multiplied by the value of each share. It also meant that the company started off with £60,000 in its bank account since the founders paid the company for their shares.

In the **second round**, they took investment from **business angels** by issuing, and selling, 40,000 new shares at £8 per share which raised £320,000. Since there were then 100,000 shares issued and all were worth £8 then the company value (after the cash was received) was £800,000. The founders retained 60% of the business whilst the investors now owned 40% of the business.

The company used that investment and made substantial progress as the company developed such that they were able to issue, and sell, another 100,000 shares at £25 per share raising £2.5m from a venture capital company in a **third round** of equity finance. This made the company worth £5m overall (since there were now 200,000 shares issued) with the founders now holding 30% of the business.

In the **fourth round**, the company floated on the Stock Exchange and at this initial public offering (IPO) issued, and sold, another 300,000 shares at £38 pounds each raising a total of £11.4m. Since the company now had 500,000 shares issued in total that gave a value for the company of £19m. The original business angel investors also sold their shares on the open market at the same time. From an original investment of £320,000 the business angels sold their shares for £1.52m — not a bad return! The founders decided to sell half of their shares (30,000) at the same time as well and so made £1.14m which was nice since they kept the other half of the shares which were also worth £1.14m. Finally, the venture capital company that had invested in round three sold approximately £2.5m worth of shares (65,790 shares) since this gave them their original investment back again whilst still having 34,210 shares in the company.

Now, of course, not all companies do as well as in this example but it does illustrate the sort of progress that can be made with 'high-growth' companies not unusual in the 'high-tech' sector. One important issue to note from this example is what happens with the founders:

- Initially, they own 100% of the business (since they own all of the shares) and that holding was valued at £60,000.

- At the second round, they raised £320,000 of equity finance but still retained overall control of the company since they held 60% of the shares. However, the value of their holding was now £480,000.

- At the third round, they raised £2.5m but their percentage holding was reduced to 30% although the value of that holding had increased to £1.5m. However, the venture capital company appointed two of its own representatives to the board of the company and invested by the purchase of 'preference' shares as opposed to the 'ordinary' shares that everyone else held. These 'pref' shares had certain rights meaning that they would get more money at liquidation than the other investors should the company go bust.

- Finally, the IPO round meant that the early investors had an 'exit strategy' and could 'get their money out' plus a healthy profit. The venture capital company took out what they had put in so that they could 're-cycle' funds into another company. The founders also made a profit but were forced by the other shareholders to retain half of their shares as an illustration of confidence in the future prospects of the company.

Now, quite obviously, this is a simplified illustration but it does give some insight into the sort of growth in share value that investors are seeking. Quite honestly, it is by no means an exaggeration since many 'early' investors want to see a very handsome return on investment — perhaps up to ten times what they invest. However, that seems reasonable since (i) they take the greatest risk by investing right at the start of a company and (ii) they recognise that they may lose all of their money if the company fails. And venture capital companies also want to see a healthy return on investment and the example here is on the low side of what they would expect. But what of the final round at IPO? Well, when the company floated on the Stock Exchange that meant that anyone (human or corporate) could buy shares. And so who owned the company changed quite radically.

This means that the Directors of the company (including the founders) had a new set of 'bosses', the shareholders, to whom they were held accountable. And investors at IPO will also be looking for an increase in share price and hence a later profit — so the company cannot stand still but has to continue to grow. Plus those investors that bought shares looking to take a share of annual profits (a 'dividend') also want the company to grow and perform well so that profits are maximised.

What does this all mean? Quite simply, that the founders and any other Directors of the company have a duty to the shareholders to maximise the return on their investment. It may have made the founders a lot of money, but it created a company that was far from a "family business"; it was a company that had to continue to grow and perform well.

Now if the company does perform well then more people will want to buy shares and perhaps less will want to sell them. Unless the company issues more shares (which it may do if it needs to raise more finance) then those shares being traded become in short supply and the share price goes up. But what happens if the company performs poorly? Well, investors then tend to sell their shares. And as more shares become available on the market then the share price tends to fall… which prompts other shareholders to sell their shares… and so a "downward spiral" follows.

All in all, getting to flotation on the Stock Exchange may never be within the scope (or plans) of a small company. Hopefully, however, this short introduction gives a useful explanation of what is involved (and what is possible) through equity finance from start to finish. **A key fact to note is that equity finance can be done via a series of funding 'rounds' as the company progresses.**

WHAT DO INVESTORS LOOK FOR?

What investors want to see is a realistic share price valuation at the outset and a clear opportunity for growth of that share price as the company develops. This means that the investor can either reckon on a healthy return from a share of the company profits each year, or can expect to sell the shares later for more than he paid for them.

Either way, implicit in this is that the investor must have a way of getting money back after the investment. How the investor will get his money back later is something that you will have to have a clear idea about before you sell any shares — this is the so-called 'exit strategy' for the investor.

THE INVESTMENT PRESENTATION

It's not by accident that we have put a lot of time into the business plan format in this book. And, once again, we are going to follow that format in the presentation that we will develop. We think that this presentation could be made to a bank manager with respect to a business loan/overdraft facility request or to a business angel for an investment presentation. The presentation can be likened to a visual tour of the Executive Summary — the last part of your plan to write.

Aim to have a presentation that lasts for no more than 30 minutes; this usually means no more than 30 slides as one per minute is quite speedy. Remember that the business plan should be no more than 30 pages? And that we are saying the presentation should be no more than 30 slides… it's all coming together now isn't it? So we can take the business plan format and re-organise it to give you the presentation format. Here is the format that we suggest would be a good starting point *(the ones underlined are the 15 key ones for a 15-minute presentation)*:

1 <u>Title slide — company name & logo</u>	2 <u>Introduction — overview of main proposal</u>
3 <u>Technology review – introduction</u>	4 Technology review — introduction
5 Technology review – introduction	6 Technology review — example
7 Technology review – example	8 <u>Intellectual Property details</u>
9 Licensing details	10 Market description — introduction
11 <u>Market description – overview</u>	12 Target products — introduction
13 <u>Target products – examples</u>	14 Competition — overview
15 <u>Competition – analysis</u>	16 <u>Commercial strategy — overview</u>
17 Commercial strategy – details	18 Market potential — overall market
19 <u>Market potential — predicted income</u>	20 <u>Management — directors/owners/partners</u>
21 Management — other key staff	22 Consultants to the business
23 <u>Production (or R&D) plan overview</u>	24 Production (or R&D) plan — first year
25 Corporate alliances – overview	26 Corporate alliances — specifics
27 <u>Resource requirements – people</u>	28 <u>Resource requirements — buildings/equipment</u>
29 <u>Resource requirements – cash</u>	30 <u>Finance sought (plus share price if equity)</u>

Have a run through before you present it for real. What we suggest with any PowerPoint presentation is that you make it **very clear and simple.** The most common mistake is to have each slide over-crowded with information — too "busy" — instead of just the key points. Use bullet points and keep to just a few per slide. The main reason for this is that only *part* of the information comes from what is on the slide — other information comes from what you say. Many skilled speakers use the PowerPoint presentation more as an aide memoire for themselves, using the bullet points to jog their memories about what they want to say. We think that this is a good technique but would suggest that you include key *points* in the bullets rather than simply using key *words*.

Avoid over-complicated tables since these seem to be a common pitfall. Generally, we advise that tables be avoided altogether if possible. This may not always be possible but do make sure that you limit their use. It's very tempting to squeeze loads of data into a table… that's the fastest way to make an investor fall asleep! If you do need a table then can you draw out any key points from the table and put into bullet format? Not always easy — but may well be worth a try.

If you are presenting at the office of the bank manager then don't expect there to be projection facilities — assume that you will be talking across a table and so have bound copies of your slides so that you and he can look at them as you talk through them. And don't give him a grotty black and white photocopy — make sure that it is in colour and properly bound. There are lots of high-street shops that will offer this service as will bigger organisations such as "Office World". Incidentally, shops such as these do a good job of making nice, bound copies of business plans and cash flow forecasts and some will even accept the file on disk. These places will also make up "standard" business cards for you quite cheaply; useful to hand out to bank managers, business angels and others even at the earliest stages of your business. Be professional from day one!

And before the meeting, don't forget to go to the toilet. And blow your nose. And have a clean hankie. Sorry… my Mum made me type this last bit.

All businesses have to plan carefully to ensure they have the right number of employees with the right mix of skills to meet their needs. There could be various reasons why a business needs to take on new staff. It might be that a member of staff has just left, or that the business is expanding and additional people are required to handle the workload. Or that a new job has come up that requires specialist skills or knowledge. Whatever the reason, you will need to go through the process of finding and employing people. This process can be both time-consuming and expensive. But it becomes even more time-consuming and expensive if you appoint the wrong people. So where to start? Define the job…

DEFINE THE JOB THAT NEEDS DOING

The first thing to do is write down a basic description of the job that needs doing. A typical job description might include the following:

- Job title — eg sales representative, office administrator, website designer

- Job objectives — be clear about what the purpose of the work is

- Reporting to (manager's title)

- Responsible for (staff for whom responsible)

- Tasks/responsibilities — list the key ones in order of priority

- Special notes — eg will the job entail working in a noisy or hazardous environment?

- A summary of the expected achievements

Employing others carries great responsibility and should not be entered into lightly

DECIDE HOW THE JOB IS TO BE DONE

Having defined what the job is, you will now have to decide on what basis the job will be done. Will you:

- Employ someone on a full-time basis? *or*

- Employ someone on a part-time basis? *or*

- Outsource it (*ie* hire a business to do it for you)?

If the job is likely to be a permanent one then it usually makes sense to employ someone to do it. Whether that person becomes a full-time or part-time employee depends on the amount of work that needs to be done. Try to quantify the time required to do the work in hours per week. Is it a full working week? There's no point paying for a full-time employee if the job doesn't demand one.

If the job is a temporary one, then you might still choose to employ someone on a full-time or part-time basis. In this case, though, the employment contract you draw up will probably be for a fixed period of time. We'll look at employment contracts in more detail later on.

The other option to employing someone is to outsource the job that needs to be done. In other words, you get another business to do the work for you. Outsourcing tends to be more expensive than employing staff. The main advantage, though, is the flexibility it gives you; you only pay for the work they actually do. Staff, on the other hand, have to be paid whether or not you have work for them!

DEFINE THE RIGHT PERSON FOR THE JOB

Now that you're clear about what the job is and how it will be done, you should ask yourself who the right person is to carry out the job competently. There is no rigid format for this **person specification** but you might want to include:

- Experience — is previous experience necessary, or can the person be trained relatively quickly?

- Qualifications — the job might require a specific educational or training qualification, eg clean HGV licence

- Skills — eg word processing, fluent Spanish, calm under pressure

- Motivation — eg does the person need to be able to work on their own?

- Special considerations — will the person have to 'put up' with anything, eg unsociable working hours, time away from home?

Please remember that you must ensure that the job description and person specification are not discriminatory in any way. We'll come back to this later in the chapter under "Your duties as an employer".

ATTRACT THE RIGHT PERSON

The question is now how you go about attracting the right person for the job. Advertising can be done internally or externally (or both).

Internal — If you already have staff on board, then this is the obvious place to start. Appointing from within has many advantages: it's cheaper, faster and there's the fact that you know the person already. Of course, if you move a member of staff from one position to another, then you're still left with a vacancy, but this might be easier to fill and less important to the business overall.

If you only have a handful of staff at the moment, then you can probably have a word with would-be candidates on an individual basis. Otherwise, you might want to advertise the position on a prominent notice board or even call a company meeting.

External — For the majority of vacancies, though, you will have to look outside your business for the right person. There are a number of options open to you:

Job centres — let your local Job Centre know what you're looking for and they'll send suitable people along for interview; the service is free and is most useful for skilled, clerical and manual jobs.

Schools and colleges — these can be a useful source of young employees. You could use the centre's careers service, participate at careers events or even offer work experience as a way of trying out interested students.

Employment agencies — these are companies who will charge a fee for finding people for your business. They usually specialise in supplying staff from particular backgrounds such as sales, accountancy, administration and personnel. Many businesses use them to get hold of temporary staff on a contract basis. Have a look through the Yellow Pages to find one that meets your needs.

There are pros and cons of using an employment agency. They have access to a source of potentially suitable candidates, and using one will save you having to advertise and respond to applications yourself, leaving you more time to do other things. The major drawback is the expense; they generally charge between 15 and 30 percent of the employee's basic salary plus a percentage of any commission/bonus paid. However, it can pay to negotiate!

Headhunters — these are similar to employment agencies but specialise in recruiting senior staff, usually executives. Often they target people working for rival firms and so the approach is made in strict confidence. A large commission is normally charged for their services — perhaps 30% of the recruit's future salary (paid by you, not the recruit).

Advertising in the media — this is probably the most common form of attracting new staff to a business. If you're considering doing this, then the

first step is to decide where you want to advertise and what your budget is. Clearly, you need to put your advert where the 'right' people will see it, so this means selecting the right newspaper, magazine or even commercial radio station. Having decided on where you want to advertise, it's now time to design the advert. Here's a checklist for what we think you should include:

- company name and logo with brief description of what you do

- job title, duties, and what is being offered (use the *job description* for this)

- skills, experience, qualifications required (use the *person specification*)

- how and when to apply eg call us on…, send your CV to…, deadline 31st March

Remember again that you must ensure that your advert is not discriminatory in any way. One way to make sure your advert looks good is to use a specialist recruitment advertising agency. They will help with copywriting and artwork, and the commission they receive should cover most of their costs without you paying more for the advert.

Internet — if you have your own website, then advertising on it is a simple and cheap way of recruiting staff. Clearly, though, its effectiveness will depend on the number and type of visitors you attract. Think of it as an additional means of finding staff rather than one that should be used to the exclusion of all others.

SHORT-LIST THE CANDIDATES

All being well, you should now start to get a stream of people applying for the job. How many and how good they are will depend not just on the quality of your advertising but also on the state of the labour market at the time. From the applications you receive, you will need to decide which ones you want to progress to interview and which you don't. This is referred to as **short-listing**.

To make the process of short-listing easier for you, you should make it clear via your advert, employment agency *etc*, how you want candidates to apply. Some employers ask for a CV (curriculum vitae), which lists a person's details and achievements. This would normally be accompanied by a letter of application, in which a candidate has the opportunity to say why they feel they would make a good employee. Other employers choose to have their own application forms so as to ensure that only relevant information is given and to make comparison between candidates easier. Here are the things a typical application form might ask for:

- Personal details — name, address, telephone number and date of birth

- Education and qualifications (including any relevant courses attended)

- Employment history — name and address of employer, time period there, key responsibilities and achievements

- Further information — this allows the applicant to write a statement in support of their application; it gives you the chance to see the style and clarity of language in the candidate's writing

- References — names and addresses of at least two 'referees' who will supply a written statement about a person's character and suitability for a job

- Declaration — so that the candidate can sign to say that the information provided is correct

One thing to watch out for in a CV or in an application form is a candidate not telling the whole truth… otherwise known as lying! Examples of things to look out for include applicants falsifying qualifications and changing dates in order to hide periods of unemployment or censor unsuccessful jobs. References should also be read with caution. Often what is not said reveals more about a candidate than what is said. And you should be suspicious if the applicant does not include their most recent employer as a referee. Do they have something to hide?

Anyway, back to the process of short-listing. You have a pile of CVs or application forms and you need to select a smaller group — the shortlist — from which the successful applicant will be chosen. This is when you can draw on your person specification again. Each application should be judged by these criteria so you might, for example, award points for each one met as a way of comparing candidates. Don't forget that you need to comply with equal opportunities legislation when selecting candidates for the shortlist.

TEST THE CANDIDATES

Having whittled the number of applicants down to a reasonable size (say six), the next step is to invite each of them along for an interview. Depending on the nature of the job, you might choose to interview them straight away or to give them some form of test first in order to assess their suitability for the role. Lots of bigger companies use quite complicated testing procedures — these can be expensive to operate. One advantage of tests however is that they yield documentary evidence about why one candidate is better suited for the job than another candidate — this can be useful in ensuring 'fair play' during the selection process. We think that there are some sensible tests that you may wish to use:

Medical test — pre-employment medical screening (or a medical examination to see whether the applicant is fit for the proposed work) may be worth considering and may also help to protect you against any claims for compensation. For example, an applicant with an allergy may not be able to work with particular substances. But be careful to ensure you are not in breach of the Disability Discrimination Act 1995; the Disability Rights Commission website (www.drc.org.uk) has useful details.

Proficiency test — this is a test to find out if a candidate can really do the job they claim to be able to do. Suppose you were recruiting a secretary. You could ask them to perform a typing test to check for speed and accuracy. Or, if the job involves using a piece of machinery, you could get the candidate to perform a particular exercise with it, *provided all health and safety issues are adequately covered.*

Psychometric test — a psychometric test is a written test, which is often used to assess the personality of a candidate. They can measure factors such as a motivation, ability to work with others, ambition and stability. They can also be used to test for general intelligence, numeracy and verbal reasoning. These tests, usually developed by psychologists, look at certain aspects of an individual's personality and can be useful in certain situations. Unless you have some familiarity with psychometric assessment it may be difficult to interpret the results and to make meaningful comparisons between individuals. There are companies that offer these services but you could simply trust your own ability to "judge character".

INTERVIEW THE CANDIDATES

It is estimated that about 90% of all organisations use the interview as their main method of selecting short-listed staff. Put simply, an interview is a face-to-face meeting between the candidate and the employer. Not only does it help you choose whether you want to employ them but it helps them choose whether they want to work for you. There are a number of issues you should consider before embarking on the interview process; remember that interviewing is a skill and, like any skill, it takes time to develop and become good at it.

OFFER THE JOB TO THE RIGHT PERSON

Now it's crunch time. You've interviewed and evaluated all the candidates and it's time to make a decision. The decision could be that there is no-one suitable for the job, in which case you will have to go back to the "attract the right person" step again and re-advertise the position. Hopefully, though, there will be one candidate that stands out above all others.

Before you make a formal offer of employment, it's best to speak to that person, either directly or through their employment agency, to confirm that they do actually want the job. And it's wise to delay sending out letters of rejection to the other candidates in the shortlist until you have a definite "yes" from your preferred choice. The offer letter itself should be conditional on receiving satisfactory references and proof of qualifications. If necessary, it may also be conditional on a pre-employment medical, providing proof of driving licence and eligibility to work in the UK.

DRAW UP THE CONTRACT OF EMPLOYMENT

By law, an employee must be given a statement of their main terms and conditions of employment within two months of commencing employment. It exists to give both you and the employee a degree of protection, certainty and security. As we touched on earlier, contracts can be either permanent or fixed-term and either full-time or part-time. Whatever the type of contract, you should include the following in it:

- Name of company and employee

- Job title

- Date when employment begins (or began)

- Place of work

- Pay scale, how payment will be made and at what intervals

- Hours of work

- Holiday entitlement

- Terms relating to notification of sickness and sick pay

- Pension arrangements

- Length of notice which an employee is entitled to receive and must give.

- Disciplinary rules, or where they can be found, and grievance procedure

The above are called 'express terms', ie they are openly agreed. There are also 'implied terms'. These are not set out in writing and not spoken of but are assumed to hold. For example, the employee is expected to exercise due care and has a duty of trustworthiness to the employer. To save you having to design a basic statement of main terms and conditions, you can download one from the ACAS website (available at www.acas.org.uk).

For senior roles you should consider including more detail within the employment contract than the minimum required by law. A senior employee, such as a company director, may well require a fairly detailed "Service Agreement" and items you might wish to cover could include restrictive covenants, confidentiality, garden leave, share options and so on. These terms may well be unfamiliar and, if in any doubt, you would be well advised to consult a professional human resource adviser or your solicitor. ***It is very important to note that the terms and conditions of employment you offer should not discriminate against part-time employees or employees working on fixed term contracts.***

A new employee may look wonderful on paper, but may not fit in or perform in the way you want them to. For this reason, it is sensible to include a probationary period in the employment contract. Typically, a **probationary period** lasts between three and six months, during which the period of notice on both sides is much reduced, eg one week. It's really there to give you and the employee the chance to test each other out. An important issue to consider when choosing to employ someone is that of pay. It is obvious that you need to offer competitive terms and conditions in order to attract and retain good employees for your business. A typical pay package might contain some or all of the following:

- Salary (or wage)

- Commission/bonus (especially for sales roles)

- Access to a pension scheme and life assurance

- Medical insurance

- Holidays in addition to statutory minimums

- Sickness pay in addition to statutory minimums

YOUR DUTIES AS AN EMPLOYER

Income tax and national insurance

The employer is responsible for collecting income tax and NI contributions from their employees on behalf of the government. The employer also has to pay a percentage of each of its employees' salaries as NI contributions itself.

For the tax year 2006/2007 that figure is 12.8% but it needs to be checked annually.

When you take on a new employee you will need to inform your local PAYE (Pay As You Earn) tax office. They will send you tax and NI tables so you can calculate what payment is due. By law you have to send the tax and NI contributions collected each month to the accounts office by the 19th of the following month. At the end of each tax year (5th April), the HMRC will send you a form asking for details of the pay and benefits of each employee. We suggest that you ask your accountant to handle these issues for you — at least in your first year of operations and perhaps longer.

Itemised pay statements

You must give your employees a detailed written pay statement when or before they are paid. By law, the statement must include:

- the amount of your employee's pay before any deductions are made

- the amount of any deductions made and what they are for

- the amount of your employee's pay after all deductions

Minimum wage

The UK introduced a national minimum wage in 1999 and details may be found at the National Minimum Wage page of the DTI website (**www.dti.gov.uk/er/nmw**). Most, but not all, workers in the UK, including home workers, part time workers, agency workers and casual workers, will be entitled to the national minimum wage.

Holiday pay and sick pay

An employee has the right to 20 days paid leave each year (bad employers may include Bank/Public holidays in this figure but we don't think that's fair). In addition, an employer must pay a minimum level of "sick pay" to most employees who are off work when ill. This is called **Statutory Sick Pay (SSP)**. SSP is paid in the same way as you would normally pay wages and you must work out and pay PAYE and NI contributions on it. It should be paid to employees who are aged 16 or over, have done some work for you under their contract, and are off sick for four or more calendar days in a row.

Working time directive

The Working Time Directive was introduced as an EC Directive under 'Health and Safety'. Its overall objective is to ensure that employees have a break from the physical task of working. The principle provisions cover:

- Limits on average weekly working time to 48 hours

- Minimum daily rest periods of 11 hours between each working day

- A right to an in-work rest break if the working day is longer than six hours

- Paid annual leave

Do note that 'Holiday Pay' and the 'Working Time Directive' both apply to 'workers' as well as employees. That means your temporary staff, as well as your employees, must be treated the same.

Maternity/paternity issues

There is a mass of legislation surrounding the rights of working parents which you need to be aware of. These include the right to maternity or paternity leave and the right for employees to claim statutory maternity/paternity pay (SMP or SPP) if they have worked for you for a certain period of time. This is a complex area — if you want to check out the latest legislation then there is a useful "Working parents" page on the ACAS website at **www.acas.org.uk/faq.html**. Your accountant will also be able to give you further information should you need it.

Discriminatory issues

At Business Boffins we think that discrimination is both evil and stupid. Hopefully that gives you a sense of where we are coming from. If that isn't enough, bear in mind that **the best person for the job is the best person for the job;** it makes no business sense to employ someone less able to do the job because of skin colour for example!

Disability discrimination — the Disability Discrimination Act 1995 makes it unlawful for employers to discriminate against current or prospective employees who have a disability or who have had a disability in the past. A disability is defined as a 'physical or mental impairment which has a substantial and long-term adverse effect on a person's ability to carry out their normal day-to-day activities'.

Regardless of how many employees you have, you have a duty to make 'reasonable adjustments' to the workplace to help the disabled person cope with their disability. ***And quite right too!***

Race discrimination — under the Race Relations Act 1976 it is unlawful to discriminate, either directly or indirectly, on the grounds of race, colour, nationality or ethnic origin. Direct discrimination occurs when you treat one person less favourably than another. Indirect discrimination occurs when you make an unjustifiable requirement, which in practice can only be met by someone from a certain race, colour, nationality or ethnic group. An example would be to say 'UK qualifications only' in a job advert.

Sex discrimination — The Sex Discrimination Act of 1975 (amended 1986) aims to avoid direct or indirect discrimination against candidates on the basis of sex. So, for example, adverts saying 'single men only need apply' or 'waitresses needed' would be regarded as discriminatory. Exceptions to this occur when there is a 'genuine occupational reason' for having a person of a certain sex, eg modelling or acting. A further important consideration is the Equal Pay Act of 1970 (amended 1983) which stipulates that women have the right to be paid equally to men for work of equal value.

It is now also illegal to discriminate against someone on the grounds of age, religion and sexual orientation.

CONCLUSIONS

The people you choose to employ will go a long way to determining the success or failure of your business. It is important to plan carefully in order to give yourself the best possible chance of finding the right person for the job you have in mind. The process begins by defining the job that needs doing (in the form of a job description), how it is to be done (employed or freelance), and who is going to do it (person specification). Careful thought should be given to the means by which you are going to attract the right people to the job. Deciding who you want to employ is completed by short-listing, and then testing and interviewing each of the candidates. Finally, it is important to be familiar with employment law when undertaking this process and drawing up a contract of employment.

If in any doubt, consult your solicitor or your human resource adviser.

Before we get into launching your business (try and be patient) there are a few things that we want to review. For starters, let's just say again that we haven't tried to turn you into an accountant or a lawyer. And there's a very good

reason for that — we believe that you should certainly engage your own accountant, and probably a lawyer too, when you start your own business. And so we haven't gone into incredible detail about taxation, National Insurance or VAT. There is no doubt that you must have a good understanding of these issues, but we recommend strongly that you let your accountant deal with that on your behalf. Most accounting firms offer a "payroll" service (calculating monthly Pay As You Earn, National Insurance, issuing payslips *etc*), and a VAT returns service, at a very competitive rate. In addition, the rules about taxation change regularly and so it is the accountant's job to keep up to date which saves you the trouble. And your accountant can file all of the necessary paperwork, on your behalf, when you start your business. Some even offer a service, for limited companies, of letting you use their office address as your company's "**registered address**". That way, all official documents from the tax man etc will go direct to your accountant — this can be very helpful and ensures that nothing gets missed by accident.

The best way to learn more about such matters is to visit the Business Link website (www.businesslink.gov.uk) and download their excellent document called "**The No-Nonsense Guide to rules and regulations for setting up your business**". Print a copy off and keep it as a reference; its over 100 pages long and so we don't expect you to read it from cover to cover at one sitting! They also produce a similar guide to raising small businesses finance. Whilst we're on the subject of Business Link, make sure that you contact your local Business Link adviser when you start in business (you can find one local to you, via their national website, by typing in your postcode). The Business Link adviser will be able to help with a number of issues outside the scope of this book. For example, they will have local knowledge about business premises that might be suitable for your business and they can help with grant applications and access to funding. Since the Business Links come under the **Regional Development Agencies** (RDAs) they will be familiar with all of the initiatives that your business could benefit from (these vary between regions).

We have tried to set out some of the key principles of business in this book and to encourage you to prepare a business plan and the associated financial plan known as the cash flow forecast. The topics that we've explained are those that we know need to be addressed by anyone starting a business. And we know that because we talked to new business owners every week about what they needed during their first year of trading; almost one hundred and fifty of them in our major field trial. This books looks at the issues around *starting* a business. The following two books in this series look at "How to Run a Successful Business" and "How to Grow a Successful Business". If you've found this book of help we hope that you might like these other books — you can find details about them at the end of this one (spot the shameless plug). The layout of this book has tried to follow a logical sequence in order to help you think through the key questions and issues that you need to address; these are:

- **What are you going to sell? What product(s) or service(s)?**

- **Do you have a market for those products and/or services?**

- **What would be the right business structure for you?**

- **Do you need to protect your ideas?**

- **What professional advisers will you need?**

- **How will you deal with tax, national insurance and VAT?**

- **What premises and equipment will your business need?**

- **What are the risks of your business and can you insure against them?**

- **What is the cash flow forecast (budget) for your business?**

- **What is your overall business plan, at least for year one?**

- **What sources of finance might you need to consider?**

- **How will you raise finance, especially start-up funds?**

- **How and when will you need to employ people?**

Many of these issues can present "go/no go" challenges prior to the launch of your business. Hopefully, you've been able to find a way through any such challenges and emerge with a robust plan that you (and also your accountant) believe can be made to work. If not, then be aware that this is not a "failure". We'd much rather you took a "no go" decision now rather than ploughing on regardless and ending up losing a lot of money. Or even your house. That would really be a failure.

We do go on a bit about planning and financial forecasting. Sorry about that. But this book is about starting a successful business. And that means planning carefully and testing out your ideas before taking the plunge. Too few people do that — which probably explains why more than half of

businesses fail within three years. Our focus on planning is therefore just the process of removing as much risk from your business before you start. Once you've done that, you can get on with launching your business. And that starts with marketing…

MARKETING YOUR BUSINESS: FRIENDS AND FAMILY

Having sold *yourself* the idea of running your own business the next target group is usually that of friends and family. And this doesn't mean selling them a product or a service. Well, not yet anyway. Here we are thinking about selling your business idea to those closest to you and who you trust the most. It is most likely that this target group will be very supportive when you sell them your idea.

Parents tend to be very proud and supportive; who wouldn't want to buy a product or service from their child or promote it to others? Spouses and partners tend to be a little more reluctant to buy the idea until they've (i) had time to think and (ii) seen some numbers from a cash flow forecast, or simple household budget, that suggest you can "make a go of it". But spouses and partners will also recognise that you've probably not enjoyed your day job for some time and that this could be a golden opportunity to get access to more of your time, especially if you'll be working from home.

And so, typically, your first real marketing communication to others will involve selling your idea to those who are closest to you. And it's likely that they will be supportive both on a personal level and perhaps also on a financial level. They may even give you your first order… "Put me down for half a dozen!" But be cautious about responses from friends and family… these are people that love you. And sometimes love can colour an opinion. Be aware then, that the response from friends and family can potentially be misleading; they are more likely to be supportive because they don't want to hurt your feelings.

So think to yourself, "was the message accurate and complete?" Or did you leave out some of the less positive aspects of your business idea? It is always important to ensure that all "marketing messages" are accurate and complete. Better to learn this lesson now, with friends and family, than find yourself sued by an unhappy customer further down the line!

MARKETING YOUR BUSINESS: THE BANK MANAGER OR INVESTOR

Next on the list is usually the bank manager. He or she is the person that you will need to sell your idea to in order to obtain an overdraft on a business account or a business loan. And so the *business plan*, the *cash flow forecast* and the *funding presentation* (as covered in earlier chapters) are in themselves marketing communication tools when you seek finance.

When selling the business idea to financiers — perhaps business angels looking to invest in your company — then it is vital to ensure that you understand you are marketing *shares* in your company. And so any funding presentation is a marketing communication and you must get your key marketing messages across to that target audience. Those key marketing messages might be:

- **You have a good business idea**

- **There is a market for your products**

- **You have planned the business well**

- **You are capable of running the business**

If you can get these marketing messages across to the bank manager, or the investor, then it is likely you will have sold them on the idea of financing you. One of the most common problems in new business start-up is that of being under-funded at the outset. It is therefore vital that you raise the start-up finance that you calculate you need before launching your business. Don't try and fudge the issue by considering taking less personal wages or by cutting back on things like marketing — this can be the start of a slippery slope. Some banks take the view that they will offer you less than you ask for, by way of a start-up loan, thinking that they are reducing their risk. In reality, they are simply *increasing* their risk of losing a reduced amount.

You should shop around and talk with different banks if your current bank is unwilling to lend the full amount that you, and your accountant, calculate that you need at the outset. On the other hand, do listen carefully to what the bank manager says are his reasons for offering you a reduced amount. It may be that you can learn something here and modify your plan accordingly. However, if your plan and budget have been approved by your accountant before you speak with the bank then you should feel confident that your "numbers" add up.

MARKETING YOUR BUSINESS: CUSTOMERS

Not surprisingly, a very important target group for your marketing messages. And a group that has the power to decide whether your business succeeds or fails. So really very, very important! Let's start by looking at a "**marketing communications**" tool that we think every business can benefit from.

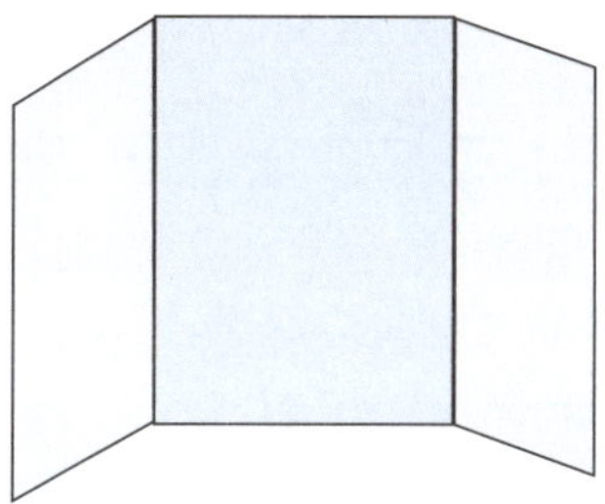

We recommend that you create a "fanfold" brochure yourself, rather than spend money on business cards and glossy brochures, when you launch your business. The fanfold brochure is no more than a single piece of A4 paper (or card) printed "landscape'" and folded twice in order to form a brochure; something like this:

If you have a colour printer then a very attractive brochure can be quite easily made once you have lined up columns of text accurately. Of course you can use a laser printer to create a brochure but that will be a little boring in just black and white. Or you could use coloured paper to liven it up a bit. Better still, try one of the pre-printed brochure 'blanks' that are available from high street office suppliers. These brochure blanks incorporate many different designs and all you have to do is ensure that your text or graphics fit into the 'blank' boxes on the template. If you have Microsoft Publisher as part of your business software then you will see that it has brochure templates suitable for launching your business although the risk here is that you might end up with something similar to a competitor — worth a thought.

Outside:

Inside Panel 1	Inside Panel 2	Inside Panel 3

Inside:

Biography Panel	Contact Panel	Front Cover

It's not easy trying to visualise the brochure but try this with a blank sheet of paper: (i) fold inside panel three over to the left, (ii) fold inside panel one over to the right.

What this achieves is that the front cover is, luckily, now at the front and when you open the brochure the biography panel is revealed under the front cover. Try it. It's easier than it sounds. OK. I know. Too much time as a child spent watching Blue Peter on television.

We suggest that the **front cover** has little more than your business name and a logo, if you have one. In fact, logos are quite easy to make using Word and the associated drawing functions — it isn't necessary to go to the expense of having a graphic artist design one for you but, of course, if funds permit then they do look better. Underneath the logo, and company name, should be a simple "**tag line**" that tells you immediately what the company is all about. If you remember "Jim's Diner" in Chapter Two, then his tag line was "Eats that taste right!" The front cover is deliberately NOT packed with information since that draws the reader to open up the brochure and find out more. When the front cover is opened, the **biography panel** is revealed. This panel should contain a photograph of the founder; *ie* you! This is not the place for a glum-looking picture — make sure that the photograph of you is one with a smile! We suggest that you provide just a couple of paragraphs about yourself including details of relevant qualifications or training (eg qualified plumber).

Having opened the front cover, it's likely that the reader will take a look at the biography panel first and then fully open the brochure to look inside. You may remember that the business plan had a single page executive summary and from that you will be able to draw some key messages for the inside of the brochure. If you have one, try to include a nice quote from a satisfied customer (even if that might be your cousin or next-door neighbour). Use a larger size of font and make the quote "jump off the page". Using a different colour will make it stand out even more. If you are using a laser printer then remember that in Word, text can be in grey as well as black — we have found that quotes in grey can look very good. Not as forceful as black and so, somehow, they don't seem too "pushy" which is something to be avoided. We think that quotes are important — a "**third-party endorsement**" is always more powerful than you saying something yourself.

The three inner panels are where you describe your business and what you offer. **Panel 1** should give some background, **panel 2** should provide information about your business and **panel 3** should detail what services and products that you offer, perhaps including "How do I find out more?" This section might say that you would visit a client to discuss requirements — in other words, make it easy for the client to purchase a product! And this last section inside the brochure refers the reader to the only panel that has not been read so far — the **contact panel**. This panel simply lists the address and the phone/fax numbers as well as a contact email address. You should also list your website (if you have one at this early stage). By the way, some people use 'info@website.com' but a personal email is better for service businesses.

USING THE BROCHURE

One of the most important lessons that a new business learns is that things don't always go according to plan. Some products sell like hot cakes whereas others, for inexplicable reasons, don't seem to sell at all. A range of services that seemed like a sensible offering can often get pruned down to a much shorter list and, conversely, new services can be added in response to customer demand. All of this argues against having glossy documents expensively produced when a business starts off. By contrast the beauty of these fanfold brochures means that they can be modified very easily as things change and printed again, with your own computer, very quickly. You would never have this flexibility if you relied on a commercial printer!

The fanfold brochure is, to our mind, a good alternative to a business card when setting off in business. It combines a way of giving contact details whilst at the same time giving a lot more information about you, the business founder, and your business products and/or services. It can also be sent out as part of a mail shot, or simply accompanying a letter, using standard envelopes.

Marketing communications are "all of those activities involved in getting your marketing messages across to target markets". Remember that what you sell will be different for different groups; you need to sell your *idea* to your bank manager in order to get a business overdraft and you need to sell *products and/or services* to customers in order to generate sales revenue. One of the secrets of effective marketing communication is to really understand who your target markets are and then develop key messages specifically for those targets. The discipline of developing a fanfold brochure is a useful exercise in honing your marketing skills and developing your key messages.

LAUNCHING YOUR BUSINESS

By now, you should have your business and financial plan sorted, your friends and family onside and any start-up finance in place. It's time to launch your business! Hang on though. Have you thought about whether you will launch on a full-time basis immediately? There is no law that says you have to work 9 to 5, for five days per week. And so is it possible to "transition" into your new business? Could you, for example, work on your new business at evenings and weekends to get started? This might allow you to benefit from an income during the daytime as an employee elsewhere. Some people even take a part-time job elsewhere (to guarantee some income) when they start up their own business. Or if they are very lucky, move to a part-time role in their old day job. It's a bit late in the day, but do have one last think about these issues before you jump into your new business full-time. Having an income stream from another source can be very useful, especially when you need time to develop any products or services. But the bad news is that working part-time elsewhere will slow down how quickly you could develop those products or services.

One thing that you can do, before you quit your old job, is to sort out things such as business premises, office equipment, insurance & pensions and so forth. A good trick here is to look at the cash flow forecast. That spreadsheet should detail all of your expenditure and it can jog your memory as to all of the things that you need to get sorted before you launch your business.

Anyway, back to the launch. It's always a good idea to have some kind of launch event; even if that is just family and friends. Because remember that family and friends will go away and spread the word about your business to their other family and friends. This "word of mouth" recommendation is a powerful marketing tool. And this is especially true within a "network" of people, such as family and friends, where recommendations are taken as trusted advice. **Always try to develop networks of contacts that can spread your marketing messages for you.** If funds permit a more elaborate launch event — such as the opening of new premises — then develop a list of people that you would like to invite. Send out invitations in plenty of time and don't forget to invite such people as your accountant and your bank manager. If your business has lots of suppliers, invite them too. You could also invite local media representatives, particularly if there is something "newsy" about what your business will be doing. And don't forget to send a copy of your newly-made fanfold brochure out with the invitations. Even if they can't attend, they'll see the brochure.

You might want to think about any special offers that could be provided at the launch event. The "Buy One Get One Free" offer (rudely known as a "BOGOFF") is a simple but powerful mechanism. The only weakness with a BOGOFF is that it suggests you must be making a huge profit in order to give things away free. It may be better therefore to have something like an "introductory 10% discount" for your products or services. Or you could consider providing a free "gift" with early purchases. Or even providing a gift to someone that recommends a client. This might seem a bit like bribery but be aware that The Institute of Directors offers a case of champagne to any member that recommends someone who buys a subscription. If they can do it, so can you! The key here is to make as big a splash as you can when you launch and then to build on that and follow up with all of the contacts that it generates.

Always remember that you are in business to sell things and make a profit.

Remember the bit at the end of "The Railway Children" film in which Jenny Agutter said, "We hope you liked it". Well ditto. We hope you've enjoyed this book and that it proves useful for you in starting your own successful business. Although we've covered a lot of ground in this book please remember that it does not contain everything you need to know about business! You will undoubtedly learn a lot about business as you go along but other, really useful, information can be obtained from the websites listed below. This list isn't exhaustive — there's a bewildering wealth of information of the internet — but it represents a "baker's dozen" sample of what we think are the really useful websites that you should be familiar with.

1	www.businesslink.gov.uk	Excellent source of business information
2	www.hmrc.gov.uk	Home of the tax man and the VAT man!
3	www.hse.gov.uk	Oodles of brilliant Health & Safety advice
4	www.companieshouse.gov.uk	Information for Ltd Companies and LLPs
5	www.ipo.gov.uk	What used to be called The Patent Office
6	www.dti.gov.uk	Department of Trade and Industry
7	www.acas.org.uk	Great site for employment guidance
8	www.drc.org.uk	Disability Rights Commission
9	www.adp.org.uk	Association of Disabled Professionals*
10	www.bvca.co.uk	British Venture Capital Association
11	www.bba.org.uk	The British Banker's Association
12	www.fsb.org.uk	Federation of Small Businesses
13	www.chamberonline.co.uk	Chambers of Commerce

** very useful website for anyone with a disability wanting to start a business*

There's just one more thing that we'd like to draw to your attention — personal safety. Launching a new business will mean that you will inevitably be arranging meetings with people that you have never met before. It is important to take steps to ensure your personal safety. For sensible and helpful advice on this matter visit the website of the Suzy Lamplugh Trust (www.suzylamplugh.org). Do it now before you forget.

Finally, we'd just like to wish you every success with your new business!

Asset: Something that is owned by the business.

Audit: The process of having your accounting records and practices inspected by an auditor, usually a qualified accountant.

Auditor: The person who inspects the accounting records and practices of your business.

Balance sheet: A financial report that gives a summary of the financial situation of the business at a given point in time.

Book value: What you estimate the value of an asset to be — usually less that was paid for it at some time later than purchase.

Brand: Typically includes a name, logo or any other visual element linking a particular product or service with a specific business.

Business Angel: High net worth (wealthy) individual who invests money in a business through the purchase of shares (see **Equity Finance**) on the basis of an expected high return on their investment within 3–5yrs.

Business premises: Your business address (see also **Registered Address**).

Business rates: Business rates are a contribution towards the cost of local authority services. The amount your business will pay depends on a number of factors including the nature of your business, the location, the property size and use.

CAMPARI model: Traditional method used to define bank lending decisions (Character, Ability, Margin, Purpose, Amount, Repayment, Insurance).

CapEx: see Capital expenditure

Capital expenditure: Any cash spent on fixed assets (see **Fixed Asset**).

Capital items: An accounting term used to describe items bought that are categorised as fixed assets (see **Fixed Asset**).

Cash flow forecast: The business budget that forecasts money coming in and out of your business on a monthly basis.

CDA: see **Confidential Disclosure Agreement**

Chairman: Usually a non-executive Company Director who chairs meetings.

Commercial strategy: How you intend to sell your product and/or service.

Confidential Disclosure Agreement: A legal document, signed by another party, stating they will not tell anyone about your idea and only use the information that you provide for a specific purpose.

Contract hire: Paying to use an item or building which is then handed back (or vacated) at the end of the rental period.

Copyright: Legal protection which automatically arises in original literary, dramatic, musical and artistic work (for example publications, recordings, computer programs and even business plans, customer lists and business letters) protecting against unauthorised copying.

Corporation tax: A tax on the company itself because the law views the company as a 'person' liable to tax on income.

Current asset: Simply anything that isn't a fixed asset that is owned by the business, eg cash in the business account or stock.

Debt finance: Using loans or an overdraft facility from a bank to fund your business. This is arranged on the condition that it is paid back at an agreed future date and that interest is paid along the way.

Debtors: Customers who have been supplied with goods or services on credit and who owe cash to the business.

Depreciation: A drop in monetary value on a fixed asset over time.

Dividend: A payment that represents a share of the company profits proportional to your shareholding in the company.

Domain name: The name of your business website, eg www.boffinswidgets.com

Due diligence: The process of checking that what you say about your business is true — often commissioned by an investor prior to buying shares in your business.

EIS: see **Enterprise Investment Scheme**

Employer's liability insurance: Compulsory for all employers insuring against death, accident or disease sustained by employees as a consequence of their employment.

Enterprise Investment Scheme: A series of tax reliefs designed to encourage investments in small unquoted companies that are EIS registered.

Enterprise: The process of doing business

Equity dividends: see **Dividend**

Equity finance: Money raised from selling shares.

Equity release: Selling shares (equity) to investors to raise finance.

Executive Chairman: Director of a company who plays a strong role in running the business overall as opposed to just chairing the meetings.

Executive summary: The ONE-PAGE brief that begins your business plan — it is the most important page!

Executive team: Those fully employed by the company and responsible for all day-to-day decisions.

Exit strategy: Mechanisms by which investors can get their money back again after a period of time (eg sales of the company or selling shares on the Stock Exchange).

External contracts: Payments made to people that have been sub-contracted.

Financial accounting: The recording of actual cash transactions (sales, purchases *etc*) and the preparation of reports.

Finished goods: Products ready for sale.

Fixed asset: Things that aren't for sale but are used as part of the business's activities in making a profit, eg equipment.

Gross salary: Total salary before the deduction of any tax or national insurance that the employee must pay.

Hire purchase: The purchase of an item over a period of time. The 'hirer' pays an initial deposit and the remaining balance (plus interest) in staged payments over a period of time.

Incubator facility: A business facility that offers rented space to new, or young, businesses under favourable terms and often with certain forms of support.

Initial Public Offering (IPO): The process of making a private limited company public by listing its shares on a stock exchange.

Intangible fixed assets: Assets of your company which lack physical substance, eg patents, copyright, trademarks.

Intellectual Property (IP): IP arises in things that that you create from your own ideas — the main forms are Copyright, Design, Patents and Trade Marks.

Investment capital: Money invested in the business.

IPO: see **Initial Public Offering**

Key person insurance: Provides money to the business to allow it to employ a replacement for the key person in the event of death or long-term illness.

Limited Liability Partnership (LLP): A partnership in which the members have limited liability for the debts of the partnership.

LLP: see **Limited Liability Partnership**

Ltd: see **Private Limited Company**

Management accounting: The use of historical data to predict future requirements and performance in order to help manage the business as it moves forward.

Marketing communications: All of the activities involved in getting your marketing message across to the target market.

Marketing mix: The four Ps of the marketing mix (Product, Price, Place, Promotion) that should be considered when planning your commercial strategy. We advise a 5th P — People!

Micro business: A small business that has less than 10 employees.

Mission statement: One sentence that captures the spirit of your business.

National Insurance Contributions (NIC): NICs build up your entitlement to certain social security benefits, including the State Pension. The type and amount of NIC you pay depends on how much you earn and whether you're employed or self employed.

Non-Executive Director: Experienced people who join the board as a director but do not have direct day-to-day management roles.

Not-For-Profit: A business that reinvests any profit it makes in doing some form of social good.

Operating expenditure: Costs associated with running the business.

Operating lease: A simple rental agreement for an item that has a resale value at the end of the lease.

OpEx: see **Operating Expenditure**

P&L: see **Profit and Loss Account**

Partnership Agreement: A document which defines how profits are to be shared between partners.

Partnership: Two or more people working together as partners.

Patent: Granted by the government giving the owner monopoly rights to an invention preventing others from exploiting it for up to 20 years.

PAYE system: "Pay As You Earn" — Accountants offer a "payroll" service where they calculate monthly tax and national insurance to be paid by the employee together with the employer's national insurance contribution.

Pref shares: See **Preference Shares**

Preference shares: Shares in a company that confer certain additional rights to the owner above those associated with ordinary shares. Often requested by Venture Capital (VC) companies.

Private Limited Company (Ltd): Limited liability for the shareholders of the company according to the capital that they invested.

Professional indemnity: A form of insurance that covers you in case you make a mistake or error when you provide advice or a service.

Proficiency test: Test to determine if a candidate can really do the job they claim to be able to do.

Profit and Loss Account (P&L): Financial tool that demonstrates how profitable the business has been over a certain period (usually one year).

Psychometric test: A written test used to assess the personality of the candidate.

Raw materials: All of those things that are bought and used to make a product.

Registered address: The address to which official mail will be delivered.

Registered design: A form of IP: protects the outward shape or appearance of industrially-made items that have significant "eye appeal".

Registered trademark: A form of IP: gives owner a limited monopoly to use a word, a logo (or something similar) to distinguish the owner's goods and services from that of competitors and to prevent others from using the same mark.

Retail price: The price of your product and/or service to the public.

Set-up capital: see **Start-up capital**

SFLG: see **Small Firms Loan Guarantee**

Share price: The value assigned to a particular portion of your business which is bought by an investor. Setting a price for shares requires professional advice.

Shareholders: People who own shares in a company.

Shareholders' Agreement: A legal document that defines such things as when shareholders can sell shares.

Shares: Generally defined by a paper certificate that details how many shares are owned by an individual.

Small Firms Loan Guarantee: An initiative from the Department of Trade and Industry (DTI) that underwrites 75% of the loan from a bank or other financial institutes for small businesses that have viable business proposals but who have failed to get a conventional loan because of lack of security.

Sole trader: A person who trades on their own as opposed to being in a partnership or as a member of a company.

SSP: see **Statutory Sick Pay**

Start-up capital: Initial funds required to start your business.

Statutory insurance: forms of insurance that are required by law.

Statutory Sick Pay (SSP): An employer must pay a minimum level of "sick pay" to most employees who are off work when ill.

Target market: The market you have defined through market research as the best place to sell your product and/or service. The term usually defines a cohort of people (eg men aged between 18–35).

Target products: The products and/or services that your business will offer.

Third party endorsement: Recommendation about your business from somebody unconnected with it.

Unique selling point: Also referred to as unique selling proposition — a feature of your product and/or service that makes you stand out against competitors.

Unit price: What it costs the business to produce one product.

Utilities: Relates to gas, water and electricity bills *etc* or may be a combined service charge from the landlord of the rented premises.

Value added tax: A form of taxation collected by business owners and paid by customers.

VAT: see **Value Added Tax**

Wholesale price: The price paid for goods bought in bulk from suppliers.

ACAS see *Advisory, Conciliation and Arbitration Service*
Accountants 18, 21, 54, 73-79, 85, 88, 95-97, 100, 103, 117, 173, 213, 221
Accounting 16, 19, 79-80, 85, 93-105, 117, 138, 163-164, 201
Advisory, Conciliation and Arbitration Service (ACAS) 196, 199, 210
Angel investors see *Raising finance*
Assets 96-118
      current assets 96-97, 99-100, 102
      fixed assets 96-97, 99, 103-104, 117
      intangible fixed assets 96
      net assets 99
Audit 88, 211
Auditors see Accountants

Balance sheet 95, 99-100, 102-105, 164, 165
Banks 21, 50, 57, 103, 177-181
      business banking 50, 131, 133, 143, 168, 177-181
      bank charges 135, 138, 140, 168
Boffins route map 17
Bookkeeping see *Basic accounting*
Book-value 96, 211
Brand 63, 154
Brochure design 205-208
Business angels see *Raising finance*
Business budget see *Cash flow forecast*
Business Link 21, 73, 172, 201
Business opportunity 150-157
Business plan 15-17, 77-81, 90, 96, 105, 109, 111-112, 120, 129, 145-167, 173-174
      components 17 , 145-166
      market research 13, 18, 21, 34-41, 43-47, 120
      writing 145-167
Business premises see *Premises*
Business profile
      Protek Dor Ltd 15
      Trinket Box 62
Business rates 110, 211
Business structure 49-61
      charities 59
      limited liability partnership LLP 53, 86
      not-for-profit 59
      partnership 51-54, 76, 84-86, 91, 105
      limited company 54-55, 158, 160, 167
      sole trader 49-60, 83, 84-86, 91, 95, 105, 107, 158-162, 167, 177, 179
Business size 5
Buying shares see *Shares*

CAMPARI model 170, 178, 211

Capital expenditure (CapEx) 103-104, 135, 141, 162, 211

Capital items 117-118

Case studies 12

Cash flow forecast 15-20, 78-79, 90, 96, 103, 105, 129, 131-167, 178-179, 188, 202-204, 209

CDA *see Confidentiality disclosure agreement*

Chairman *see Management*

Charities *see Business structure*

Commercial strategy 152-153

Companies House 54, 58-59, 74, 86, 88, 91, 93

Company director *see Management*

Company secretary *see Management*

Competition 152

Confidentiality disclosure agreement (CDA) 64, 66

Consultants *see Management and also Professional advisers*

Contract hire *see Leasing*

Copyright *see Intellectual property*

Corporate alliances *see Operating plan*

Corporation tax 87, 91, 103, 124

Creating a brochure 205-208

Current assets *see Assets*

Death in service scheme 124-127, 137

Debt finance charges *see Banks*

Debt finance *see Raising finance*

Debtors 97, 100, 102, 211

Department of Trade and Industry 210

Depreciation 96, 101, 118, 211

Design right *see Intellectual property*

Directors *see Management*

Dividend 55, 87, 91, 101-104, 175, 186, 212

Domain name 76, 150, 212

DTI *see Department of Trade and Industry*

Due diligence 174, 212

eBay 18

Employing people 189-200

    contract of employment 196-197

    employer duties 197-200

    employer's liability insurance 121, 212

    employment agencies 191-192

    interviews 195

    job advertising 191-193

    job description 189-190

    recruiting 189-195

    proficiency test 195, 213

    psychometric test 195, 213

    short-listing 193-194

    statutory sick pay (SSP) 198, 214

Enterprise 9, 73, 219, 212

Enterprise investment scheme (EIS) 57

Equipment 14, 19-20, 26, 79, 104, 107-119, 122, 137, 144, 161, 165, 176

Equity finance *see Raising finance*

Equity release *see Shares*

Executive Chairman *see Management*

Executive summary 148

Executive team *see Management*

Exit strategy 56, 175, 185, 187

External contracts 134, 163, 212

Finance leasing *see Leasing*

Finance assets *see Assets*

Financial accounting 94, 212

Financial adviser *see Independent Financial Adviser*

Finished goods 97, 212

First Aid *see Health and safety*

Financial management 93-94

Front cover (of business plan) 146-147

Fixed price services *see Pricing*

Financial analysis *see Operating Plan see also Cash flow forecast*

Funding presentation *see Investment presentation*

Gross salary 137, 212

Health and safety 81, 109, 113-115
     health and safety advisers 81
     Health and Safety Executive 81, 113-115

Hire purchase 118

HM Revenue and Customs 94

Hotels *see Premises*

Hourly rates *see Pricing*

HSE see Health and Safety Executive

Human resource advisers 81, 197, 200

Incubator facilities *see Premises*

Independent Financial Adviser 21, 74, 79, 81, 109, 127, 129

Initial Public Offering (IPO) 56, 184, 212

Insurance 119-129

Intangible fixed assets *see Assets*

Intellectual property 61-71, 81, 150, 164, 183
     copyright 63, 66-67, 71, 146
     registered designs 63, 71
     patents 16, 18, 20, 63-71, 76, 81, 150, 164, 182, 210
     registered trademarks 63, 65, 71
     trademarks 65

Introduction to business plan 149-150

Inventions *see Intellectual property*

Investment presentation 187

Investment *see Raising finance*

Key person insurance 125, 212

Lawyer 54-60, 76,
Leasing 13, 111, 118
      contract hire 118
      finance leasing 118
      operating lease 118
Licensing 113, 145, 150, 187
Limited company *see Business structure*
Limited liability partnerships *see Business structure*
Loan *see Raising finance*

Management 157-159
      accounting 94, 213
      chairman 159, 211
      consultants 159
      directors 58-59, 158-159
      executive chairman 159, 212
      executive team 212
      key managers 159
      owners 158-159
      partners 158-159
Managers *see Management*
Market description 151
Market potential 154-157
Market research 35-48
Marketing communications 205, 208, 213
Marketing mix 153
Marketing your business 203-209
Micro business 11
Mission statement 148

Non-disclosure agreement (NDA) *see Confidentiality disclosure agreement*
Not-for-profit *see Business structure*
National insurance 19, 21, 50, 77, 83-93, 137, 141, 197
Non-executive directors *see Management*
Net assets *see Assets*

Offices *see Premises*
Operating lease *see Leasing*
Operating plan 145, 160-163
      corporate alliances 161-162
      expenditure (OpEx) 103, 135, 141, 162, 213
      production plans 160-161
      research and development 160-161
      resource requirements 162
Ordinary shares 213
Overdraft *see Raising finance*

Oxford Capital Partners 15

P&L *see Profit and Loss*
Partnership agreement 52, 54, 85-86, 158, 213
Partnerships *see business structure*
Patent agent 67, 69, 70-71, 81
Patent application 65, 69-70
Patent office *see UK Intellectual Property Office*
Patents *see Intellectual property*
PAYE 85, 87, 91, 198
Preference shares 213
Premises 14, 16, 19, 21, 35, 76-79, 107-118
    hotels 112
    incubator facilities 110
    offices 110
    restaurants 112
    shops 112
    warehouses 111-112
    workshops 111-112
Pricing 155-157
    fixed price services 156
    hourly rates 155
    retail price 39, 40, 214
    strategies 155
    unit price 38, 214
    wholesale price 39-40, 214
Private limited company *see Business structure*
Product liability insurance *see Insurance*
Professional advisers *see Accountant, Health and safety adviser, Independent financial adviser, Lawyer, Patent agent, Recruitment consultant*
Professional indemnity insurance *see Insurance*
Proficiency test *see Employing people*
Profit and Loss (P&L) 100-101
Protecting your business *see Intellectual property*
Protek Dor Ltd 9
Psychometric test *see Employing people*
Public liability insurance *see Insurance*

Raising finance 177-188
    Business Angels/angel investors 57-58, 79
    Debt finance 20-21, 131-132, 163, 167, 169-171, 176-181, 187, 204, 208
    Venture Capitals 20, 57, 172, 174, 184, 185
    Venture Capital Trusts 57
Raw materials 20, 34, 97, 133-135, 139, 157, 161, 213
Registered address 107
Registered design *see Intellectual property*
Registered trademark *see Intellectual property*
Recruitment consultant 81

Research and development plans *see Operating plan*
Resource requirement *see Operating plan*
Restaurants *see Premises*
Retail price *see Pricing*
Risk 119-130

Sales 11, 23, 35-36, 43, 88-89, 94-95, 101, 103, 134-136, 139, 144, 151-154, 157, 163, 165, 177, 208
Selling shares *see Shares*
SFLG *see Small firms loan guarantee scheme*
Shareholders' Agreement
Shares 56-58, 79, 87, 127, 140, 167, 172, 175-177, 181-187, 204
Shops *see Premises*
Small firms loan guarantee scheme (SFLG) 172
Sole trader *see Business structure*
Solicitors 16, 64, 73-75, 77
Start-up funding/capital 20, 50, 55, 177, 214, 144, 166 *see also Raising finance*
Statutory Sick Pay (SSP) *see Employing people*

Target market 37, 208, 214
Target products 151
Tax 16, 19, 21, 49-50, 54, 57, 77, 79, 80, 83-92, 103, 121, 124, 127, 176, 197-198, 201-202, 210
Technology review 149
The Trinket Box 61
The Valuation Agency 108
Third party endorsement 214
Trademark *see Intellectual property*

UK IPO *see UK Intellectual Property Office*
UK Intellectual Property Office (UK IPO) 210, 222
Unique selling proposition 174, 214
Unit price *see pricing*

Valuation Agency *see The Valuation Agency*
Value Added Tax 16, 19, 21, 24, 79, 83-92
VAT *see Value Added Tax*
VCs *see Venture Capital*
VCTs *see Venture Capital Trusts*
Venture Capital *see Raising finance*
Venture Capital Trusts *see Raising finance*

Ward, Joanne 61, 62, 62
Warehouses *see Premises*
Workshops *see Premises*
Writing a business plan *see Business plan*
Wholesale price *see Pricing*

Regional Resource Centre for Advanced Technology

The Science & Technology Facilities Council is proud to host the Regional Resource Centre for Advanced Technology at its Rutherford Appleton Laboratory on the Harwell Science and Innovation Campus in South Oxfordshire.

The Regional Resource Centre for Advanced Technology (RRC) is one of five Regional Resource Centres funded in the South East region. Other RRCs include Biotechnology and Healthcare (Kent); Environmental Technologies (Kent); Marine Technologies (Southampton); and Aerospace and Space Technologies (Farnborough).

The RRC for Advanced Technology provides a focal point for gaining knowledge about how to optimise scientific and technological developments in the areas of Advanced Instrumentation, ICT and Electronics, and how best to upskill staff to understand and develop products which will meet the requirements of tomorrow's advanced technology.

Working in partnership with Pera and The Precise Group and co-financed by SEEDA and the European Social Fund, the RRC for Advanced Technology will work with other regional education and training providers to offer pioneering industry-driven training modules for companies and individuals in the advanced technology sector across the SEEDA region.

This exciting project will address the training needs of businesses and provide specialist technological skills and expertise. The project will provide a clear and structured career pathway for technology based careers to boost the skills base in the South East and strengthen our position in the advanced technology market.

Eligible businesses and individuals will receive funded training support focusing on advanced skills that are critical to businesses. The project also aims to focus on raising awareness of science and technology across the region, and will, through seminars, open events, lectures and tours, work not only with local businesses but also with schools, FE colleges, universities, research institutions and the general public to promote science and technology awareness and education.

To find out how you and your staff can receive specialist funded training in Instrumentation, ICT and Electronics, please contact:

Jan Lawrence, Project Coordinator

Regional Resource Centre for Advanced Technology

CCLRC Rutherford Appleton Laboratory

Chilton, Didcot, Oxfordshire, OX11 0QX, UK

T: +44 (0)1235 445995

E: rrc@rl.ac.uk   www.RRCTechnology.co.uk

Other Regional Resource Centres

RRC for Biotechnology and Healthcare - www.kentscienceresourcecentre.co.uk

RRC for Environmental Technologies - www.rrcets.co.uk

RRC for Aerospace/Space - www.aerospacerrc.co.uk

RRC for Marine Composites - www.marinerrc.co.uk

Barclays Bank PLC

Barclays Local Business aims to champion small businesses and prides itself on the level of service and range of support that we offer to people who are starting up in business. We even make sure our start-up customers get free time with a local accountant, solicitor and marketing professional making sure they have all the support they need.

For further information contact Richard Huddleston on 0845 6052345

Oxford University Begbroke Science Park
Centre for Innovation and Enterprise

At Begbroke Science Park high-tech start up companies flourish alongside University academics. The Centre for Innovation and Enterprise offers serviced office and laboratory accommodation, the Institute of Advanced Technology houses researchers from 5 science Departments and companies and academics from across the UK use the Oxford Materials Characterisation Service.

For further information contact Professor Peter Dobson, Dr Caroline Livingstone or Ms Barbara Allsworth on 01865 283700 or go to www.begbroke.ox.ac.uk

Begbroke Science Park is located at Sandy Lane, Yarnton, Oxon, OX5 1PF
Fax: 01865 374992

HR Advantage

At Begbroke Science Park high-tech start up companies flourish alongside University

HR Advantage is a leading human resource services company. Our job is to help organisations achieve their objectives through their people - everything from on call advice and guidance to full HR outsourcing. We are expert, practical, good to work with and cost effective. See more at www.hradvantage.co.uk, or call us on 01494 451681.

For further information please contact Campbell Ritchie on 01494 451681 or go to www.hradvantage.co.uk

HR advantage is located at Unit 9 Lancaster Court, Coronation Road, Cressex Business Park, High Wycombe, Bucks, HP12 3TD
Fax: 01494 524637

Experian

Experian is a global leader in providing analytical and information services to organisations and consumers to help manage the risk and reward of commercial and financial decisions.

Combining its information tools and deep understanding of individuals, markets and economies, Experian partners with organisations to establish and strengthen their customer relationships.

For further information please contact Andrew Davis on 0115 968 5619 or go to www.experian.co.uk.

Experian is located at Embankment House, Electric Avenue, Nottingham, NG80 1EH.
Fax: 0115 968 5662

Focus

FOCUS Independent Financial Advisers and Independent Insurance Consultants

FOCUS help protect businesses and their assets by arranging bespoke business insurance packages and reducing risk factors.

FOCUS also provides impartial guidance on securing the financial future for the business owners, retaining and growing their wealth, assisting in the prosperity process.

Focus Independent Financial Advisers is authorised and regulated by the Financial Services Authority

For further information contact Rob Evans or Phil Casey on 01865 813306 or go to www.focus-oxford.co.uk

Focus is located at Seacourt Tower, West Way, Oxford, Oxfordshire, OX2 0JL

HW, Chartered Accountants

HW, Chartered Accountants is a top 20 firm with national coverage and local offices, whose partners specialise in advising growing businesses so that they operate as efficiently and profitably as possible. Our services include providing advice on accounting systems, business structures and tax strategies, from start-up through to exit planning.

For further information contact Rodney Style at HW Oxford on 01865 378282 or email rhstyle@hwca.com

Haines Watts is located at Sterling House, 19/23 High Street, Kidlington, Oxford, OX5 2DH
Fax: 01865 377518

James Cowper

As Accountants and Business Advisers our main areas of specialisation include business direction, business assurance, outsourcing, corporate finance, business tax and private client tax. A diversity of companies and individuals seek our advice and guidance in industries ranging from rural and bloodstock to technology and inward investment.

With an excellent record for retaining clients for many years – a testament to our refreshingly creative way of looking at challenges and opportunities – whatever your accounting or business advisory needs, we offer real results.

For further information contact Sue Staunton on 01865 200500, email sstaunton@jamescowper.co.uk or go to www.jamescowper.co.uk

Jennings of Garsington Ltd

We run business premises to the East of Oxford. We specialize in premises for small and start up businesses and offer a relaxed approach which removes the stress of property rental. Both working directors have been trained as business advisors and our caring approach enables our tenants to prosper on our parks.

For further information contact Mike Jennings on 01865 893300 or go to www.jennings.co.uk

Jennings of Garsington is located at Hampden House, Monument Business Park, Chalgrove, Oxford, OX44 7RW Fax: 01865 893333

Market Engineering

Market Engineering is one of Europe's leading Press Relations and marketing communications agencies for innovation businesses. With five engineers in-house, many of whom also have post-graduate marketing qualifications, we are able to deliver accurate marketing communications programmes that will help you grow your sales and add value to your business.

For further information contact Richard Gotch on 01295 277050 or go to www.marketengineering.co.uk

Market Engineering is located at North Bar House, North Bar, Banbury, OX16 0TH
Fax: 01295 277030

Manches LLP

MANCHES

Manches can provide all of the legal advice that a young business needs: on business structures, intellectual property protection and exploitation, employment issues and property ownership and occupation.

Our aim is to understand your business and its requirements and to build a long term relationship with you.

For further information please contact Patrick Baddeley on 01865 722106 or go to www.manches.com

Manches LLP is located at 9400 Garsington Road, Oxford Business Park, Oxford, OX4 2HN
Fax 01865 201012

The UK Intellectual Property Office (UK – IPO)

The UK Intellectual Property Office (UK – IPO) is the government body responsible for the establishment and maintenance of the national framework of intellectual property rights (IPR) (patents, designs, trade marks and copyright) and the granting and management of rights within that framework.

The UK Intellectual Property Office is an operating name of the Patent Office.

For further information please contact Sally Long on 01633 814163 or go to www.ipo.gov.uk

UK-IPO is located at Concept House, Cardiff Road, Newport, NP10 8QQ
Fax 01633 814590

Professor Russell Smith began his career in business by starting an electronics company, whilst still a student, in the early 1980's. Products from that company were promoted by the British Council and were sold in 27 countries worldwide. In 1986 he joined the pharmaceutical industry and led drug development programmes for multi-national companies in North America, Europe and Japan.

Russell founded Business Boffins Ltd in 1998 to create business support programmes aimed at sustainability, for the small business community, in conjunction with Oxford Brookes University Business School and a range of professional advisers. The programme developed by Russell has now become an accredited university course that offers a new Certificate in Small Business Management. A major trial of the programme with nearly 150 businesses over one year saw business failure rates dramatically reduced.

Over the last six years, Russell has worked with a number of organisations that seek to promote enterprise and provide support to new business owners. He has a particular interest in 'reaching the hard to reach' and has developed various schemes aimed at making education and self-employment support available for disadvantaged groups with an emphasis on the disabled, those with caring responsibilities and ex-forces personnel who leave the services following injury or ill health.

Russell is married with four sons and lives in Oxfordshire. In his spare time he enjoys long distance walking, painting watercolours, making furniture from native British hardwoods and any excuse to do some welding — including making cars from scratch for his sons. He writes a monthly page on business matters for "The Independent" newspaper and lectures extensively — recent international lecture tours include Iceland, Finland, Estonia, Latvia and Italy.

You can order further copies of this book direct from Boffins House Publishing.

FREE UK DELIVERY!

To order further copies of "How to Start a Successful Business" please send a copy of this form to

> **Business Boffins Ltd**
> **Dairy Barn**
> **Belcher's Farm**
> **High Street**
> **Little Milton**
> **Oxfordshire**
> **OX44 7PU**

Alternatively you can buy online at www.businessboffins.com
or call us on 01844 278448.

Please send me ___ copies of How to Start a Successful Business

❐ I enclose a UK bank cheque or postal order, payable to Business Boffins Ltd
for £______ at £14.99 per copy.

NAME _______________________________________

ADDRESS _______________________________________

____

____

____

POSTCODE _______________________________________

Please allow 28 days for delivery and please do not send cash. Offer subject to availability. Please tick box if you do not wish to receive further information from Business Boffins ❐